the
SUCCESSFUL
Struggle

POWERFUL TECHNIQUES
TO ACHIEVE
ACCELERATED RESILIENCE

Courtney Clark

Incline Ink
Austin, Texas

THE SUCCESSFUL STRUGGLE
© 2016 Courtney Clark
Austin, Texas
SuccessfulStruggle.com

Book design by TLC Graphics, *www.TLCGraphics.com*
Cover: Tamara Dever
Interior: Erin Stark
Editor: Lari Bishop
Proofreader: Alexandra O'Connell

ISBN: 978-0-9970093-0-9
Library of Congress Control Number: 2016901113
Printed in the United States of America

To the ones in my life who have been there
for both the successes *and* the struggles:
none of this is possible without you.

———

CONTENTS

INTRODUCTION

AT 26 YEARS OLD, I BELIEVED I WAS INVINCIBLE.

You've probably experienced that feeling of being invincible at some point in your life, too. Most of us can remember a time when we felt like nothing could touch us, and everything we wanted could be obtained through a simple combination of hard work and luck. We were charmed. Life was good. Anything was possible.

Earlier that year, the year I still believed I was invincible, I had moved across the country, bought a house, and landed a prestigious new job with a local nonprofit agency. After a particularly harried month of work and volunteer events, I knew I needed to get away for a weekend of relaxation, so I booked a trip to a beautiful spa a few hours away. I planned a lovely long weekend of yoga, hiking, and massages to try to shake off the stresses of my busy life. I even turned off my cell phone, to complete the happy illusion of having truly "escaped" the real world for a short while.

My getaway was a success! I left the spa after three days in a complete state of rejuvenation and bliss. I had gotten so relaxed, in fact, that I forgot my phone was still turned off. I made the entire two and a half hour drive home in silence, never once giving a thought to the phone that was tucked away in my bag, its screen dark. It wasn't until I was turning onto my street that I realized I had never turned it back on. Grudgingly, I reached into my purse and hit the power button. The phone churned to life as I pulled into my driveway. As I was walking through the door, the phone pinged in my hand, alerting me to a message.

As I listened to the voice mail, it didn't occur to me to be alarmed by the words I was hearing. I didn't realize, back then, that when your doctor, whom you had recently visited for a routine dermatology exam, calls at 9pm on a Sunday night and leaves an urgent-sounding voice mail to call her back immediately, that you **should** be alarmed! So I punched in her number, completely oblivious to the fact that my life was about to change.

As she spoke, I suddenly realized I was no longer invincible. I had cancer.

Over the next few days, I became an expert on things I never thought I would even need to know about. I learned what malignant invasive melanoma meant. I learned about treatment methods, surgical techniques, and medical options. I researched doctors and hospitals. I finally learned how my health insurance actually worked! And I learned things about myself too, like how I would react when it became clear that my very life was being threatened.

When my surgeon took out the tumor, he also removed two nearby lymph nodes to check for cancer. For 10 days I waited as they dissected those lymph nodes, looking for any sign that the cancer had spread. Metastatic melanoma is a devastating disease, and I sat up in bed those 10 nights, wishing for sleep but knowing it wouldn't come until I had some good news.

When the call from my doctor came in I hesitated before picking up. My heart was pounding in my ears as I reluctantly answered. But my doctor's voice on the other end of the line was happy, and the news was good. The surgery had gotten it all, and I was cancer-free. Life was good. For now.

Looking back on that day, the day my illusion of invincibility was shattered, I realize now that none of us is bullet-proof. Life is filled with moments of challenge. Struggle is unavoidable. Job security isn't guaranteed. We get ill. We fight with our families. A raise and promotion go hand in hand with longer hours and more stress.

When life doesn't go the way we expect, we're often knocked off balance. Have you ever caught yourself saying, "Why is this happening to me?!" If so, you're not alone. In fact, almost everyone I've spoken to on this topic has had that exact same thought. The answer is that it happens to a lot of people. **Everyone struggles at some point in life.**

In those moments when we feel like we've somehow lost the path we're supposed to be on, and life has become extra-challenging, we look for ways to set the world right again. Resilience-building techniques have become a focus of research, articles, and books over the past several years as all of us look for ways we can buffer ourselves against the struggles of life. We're on a hunt for strategies to continue to succeed at life and at work.

If you've ever turned to a friend for advice on how to bounce back after a struggle, or found an internet article on the topic, you'll be familiar with a lot of these techniques: Meditate. Volunteer. Adopt a pet. Lean on a friend. Avoid venting. Don't blow things out of proportion.

All of these techniques certainly do build resilience. I have used them often, as ways to get over my own struggles. But there's something interesting about these techniques. While they're all valuable, they aren't quite all created equal. They don't all work the same way or solve the same problems. Specific tactics, research shows, work well for specific types of situations, struggles, and stressors. Likewise, specific tactics clearly **don't** work in other situations. They are all useful, but not *interchangeable*.

If you don't understand how to apply the right resilience tools to the particular challenging situation at hand, you run the risk of frustration when the tactics you try don't work. The more you try and fail, the more helpless you feel, until you eventually give up.

In this book, you will learn how to determine which type, or state, of struggle you are experiencing, which coping strategies are the best match for that struggle, and how to deploy those specific strategies to be at your most resilient. By matching the struggle you are experiencing to the right resilience strategies, you will achieve accelerated resilience, and be able to recover from times of struggle more quickly. You will, in essence, have a more successful struggle.

Using The Right Tool at the Right Time

The word "coping" is off-putting to some people. Coping can be perceived as negative, such as when you say someone is "merely coping" with a situation. It's true that coping and resilience can appear very different to an outside observer, because "coping" seems to connote an ongoing, laborious struggle, while "resilience" is perceived as describing a near-instantaneous recovery.

But even those people who exhibit extreme resilience, and bounce back quickly, do so using coping tactics. In fact, it's their effective and prompt use of these powerful techniques that allows them to be resilient in the first place. Resilient people don't bypass coping completely, they just don't linger there very long. To put a prompt end to your struggle, you must cope effectively and quickly.

Focusing on the wrong resilience strategies, however, not only doesn't help us, it can actually set us back. When we deploy a technique that doesn't pay off, we can begin to feel like nothing will work. We worry that life might never return to normal again.

For accelerated resilience to occur, we must select the right resilience tool for each job. The powerful techniques in this book are designed to move you from struggle to success in the shortest amount of time possible. In today's world, we don't have time to solve our struggles slowly. We don't just need resilience; we need accelerated resilience to recover as quickly as possible. The two figures below show the difference between resilience trajectories when the strategies are applied correctly and when they are not.

MODEL 1.1

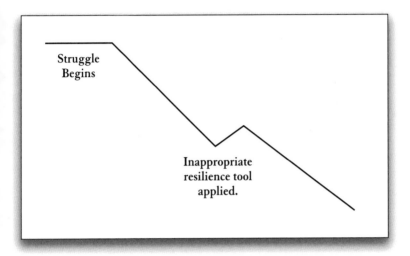

MODEL 1.2

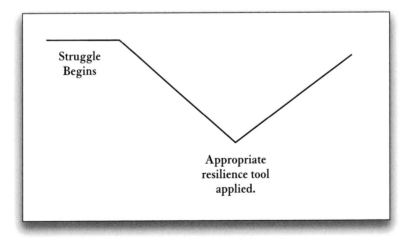

Following my cancer diagnosis and subsequent surgery, I tried to shake off the experience and go back to being a normal 26-year-old. Many things about my life were the same: I was still working at a nonprofit organization, I still had lots of adopted dogs waiting for me at the end of every day, and I still blasted Broadway show tunes during my commute (don't judge!). But I made a lot of changes, too. I moved to a new city and took a job at a young adult cancer survivor support nonprofit. I started dating again, after the breakup of my previous relationship following the cancer. I quickly started mentoring other young adults with a diagnosis of melanoma like mine.

It was a full year, however, before I realized that my zealous pursuit of "normal" was leading me to a dead end. At the end of the day, I still found myself feeling vulnerable and sorry for myself. I was stuck feeling like a victim. I was working at the cancer non-profit full-time, helping other young adults navigate the crazy waters of diagnosis, treatment, and recovery when the founder (my boss) sent me to speak at an event a few hours away, presenting to a room full of doctors and survivors. I talked about the mission of our organization and told a little bit of my story. Mostly, I tried to inject plenty of humor into the situation, and was even able to laugh about my diagnosis and the ways my life had changed since then.

When I finished speaking, two women walked up to me. The mother introduced herself first, with tears in her eyes. Her daughter, she told me, had been diagnosed four months earlier. They had been fighting for weeks about every little thing: whether the daughter could safely go out with friends, what kind of treatment should she choose, etc. The mother then told me, and the daughter confirmed, that the cancer diagnosis had been tearing their relationship apart. The mother looked at me and grabbed my hand:

"Everything I heard you say is what she's been telling me. I wasn't listening to her, I didn't understand," she whispered. "I'm so glad you were here today. Now I get it. Now I know how I can support her."

Whether anyone else heard what I said that day or not, I changed two lives. And I changed my own perspective on my diagnosis as well. Instead of feeling sorry for myself, I felt grateful that I had the opportunity to smooth the path for somebody else, based on my own struggle. My cancer finally had a payoff, a deeper meaning.

For months I had been relying on survival tactics that had worked for me before, to get over things like breakups, big changes at work, or losing a job. But none of them had worked this time, and they just left me more and more frustrated. At last, I had found the tactic designed to work for exactly this moment—finding the silver lining.

Finding the right resilience tactic is a little bit like trying to accomplish household chores at my house. I'm now married to a wonderful man. But... every single time I ask my husband for a household fix, he cheerfully walks up to me with his electric rechargeable screwdriver. Using that screwdriver is quick and easy. That screwdriver does solve a lot of problems in our house, like when a nail just isn't big enough to hold the new painting we bought at a nonprofit auction. But sometimes, I just need him to bring the darn hammer. Or the saw. If my husband could, I think he would mow the lawn with the electric screwdriver!

Though you wouldn't know it to watch my husband around the house, we do have more than one tool in the toolbox out in our garage. And they all come in handy for their different tasks. In the same way, your resilience is like a toolbox. When you are faced with a problem that's dragging you down, you don't need just any tool, you need exactly the right tool. This book is designed to help you not only stock your toolbox full of techniques, but also to help you learn how to reach in and pick out exactly the one tailored to the specific challenge at hand. No matter what situation or struggle is draining your resilience, you'll be able to fix it with the appropriate techniques for the job.

By the end of the book, you may decide to retire some techniques you've been relying on that aren't working for you. Or you may decide to put them on hiatus, and only pull them out for the specific situations where they're prescribed. And it can be hard to part ways with resilience strategies on which you've relied for years! They sometimes feel like old friends. But the wrong techniques matched with the wrong situations can hinder you, so if you find you've been relying on the wrong strategy all along, don't dwell on it. Just work to move forward and start turning the new tactics into a habit.

Two Types of Techniques— And Why You Need Both

Sometimes when we struggle, we're actually struggling on two different fronts. We have the original root cause of the struggle, or the problem. That's usually something external to us, like something that happened in our environment or something that someone else is doing that is causing the struggle. But we can also be challenged by our own emotions and responses, which becomes a secondary struggle. The way we instinctively respond to a situation can sometimes make us feel worse!

Because we may be struggling on two fronts, you'll see that many of the solutions in this book are designed to help you cope in two ways. Problem-focused coping is one of the most commonly suggested ways to cope with any kind of struggle. Problem-focused coping means coming up with a solution that gets at the heart of the issue, and that – hopefully – ultimately corrects or remediates the underlying problem. Problem-focused coping is an active strategy, and the goal is that it fixes the cause of your struggle.

But not all struggles can be fixed, or they can't be fixed right away, and the lack of a quick solution can cause us to slide even more deeply into our struggle. Studies show that when problem-focused coping doesn't completely solve a problem, emotion-focused coping becomes important, as well. Emotion-focused coping is aimed at addressing the feelings and reactions you have to the problem. In other words, the aim of emotion-focused coping is to make you feel better whether the problem is fixed or not.

Problem-focused coping and emotion-focused coping may feel like two completely different tactics, but you can and should make them work together. Problem-focused coping is appropriate and effective in the workplace, but we tend to deal with turmoil in our personal lives with a more emotional approach. Some people may feel that they are more inclined to use one type of technique over the other, because of their personality. But research shows that all of us, no matter our nature, need to have a wide variety of these tools at our disposal. Your application of any given strategy may be unique to you, but the techniques work regardless of who you are and how you prefer to behave. The bottom line is, both types of techniques can (and should!) be performed both at work and at home. In many sections of this book, you'll see that combining both problem-focused and emotion-focused tactics leads to more effective handling of the situation than using only one or the other.

Six States of Struggle

You may have a habitual way you usually react when you are under stress. Maybe you lash out at others, or maybe you retreat into silence. We often fall into the same patterns when we're under stress, even if the cause is different every time. In order to actually address the root cause of the stress and find resilience, however, you need to know what kind of stress you are facing.

This book addresses six major states, or types, of struggle. Each has a specific cause, makes you behave in certain ways, and threatens your well-being for different reasons. And because the root cause of each of the six states of struggle is different, the tactics you need to use are unique for each. If choosing the "right" resilience techniques means matching them to the struggle you're experiencing, it's essential that you know what struggle you're experiencing.

The six states of struggle are *change, chaos, conflict, rejection, illness and injury*, and *powerlessness*. We struggle with *change* when it is unexpected, unwanted, or so massive that it causes upheaval. *Chaos* is the experience of being overwhelmed, too busy, and frantic. *Conflict* occurs when we have clashing beliefs or values with another person that cannot be easily resolved. *Rejection* is the experience of being unwanted, excluded, or blocked from a desire or goal. Physical struggles like *illness and injury* can threaten our very lives, as well as our capabilities to carry on the way we used to. Finally, *powerlessness* is a struggle that can arise out of any of the other five struggles, when our attempts to correct what's going wrong in our world have failed, and we begin to feel we have no control over our challenges.

Sometimes it's obvious which of the six states of struggle you're in, but sometimes it isn't so clear. Struggle often just feels like struggle, when we're in the middle of it. We're stressed, we're angry, we're totally consumed. No matter what caused it, we just feel like we're dangling at the end of our rope. When we're stressed, we're not seeing things in a simple way. Everything tends to roll together and get complicated, clumping up into one giant feeling of stress.

So how can you tell which state you're in?

If you're feeling:
depressed, hopeless, helpless, and not in control

You might be experiencing:
powerlessness

If you're feeling:
confused, upended, out-of-sorts, and like you don't
know your place in the world anymore

You might be experiencing:
change

If you're feeling:
overwhelmed, overloaded, exhausted, or burned out

You might be experiencing:
chaos

If you're feeling:
angry, irritated, and offended, particularly directed
at a single person or group

You might be experiencing:
conflict

If you're feeling:
unimportant, unsuccessful, unwanted,
excluded, or heartbroken

You might be experiencing:
rejection

If you're feeling:
like your life is threatened, your health is bad,
and you're facing your mortality

You might be experiencing:
illness or injury

Knowing what struggle you're experiencing helps you resist the kind of rash reactions that can negatively impact you and the people around you. If you're starting to feel stressed because of changes at work, but you haven't yet recognized it for what it is, you might find yourself being ill-tempered with your friends and family. Or perhaps you're becoming less solution-oriented at meetings with your colleagues. Identify the struggle as soon as you start to feel some of the signals listed on the previous page, and take action. When you deploy your resilience strategies in a timely manner (if they're the **right** strategies!) you can work your way out of the struggle before it takes its toll on you and the people around you.

One common struggle this book does not address is grief. Grief is the feeling that arises from a situation of loss, and it has been widely written about. While grief can indeed be an incredible struggle, this book focuses on six other types of struggle because grief is a state people **expect** you to struggle with. You are less likely to be expected to "snap out of" grief, whereas with many other struggles you are called on to "just deal with it." Accelerated resilience is not expected, nor necessarily possible, when confronted with grief.

The first struggle we're going to explore is powerlessness. Powerlessness is unique because it is actually a secondary state that can often occur when you get stuck for too long in any of the other struggles. We need to start with it, however, because if you're stuck in powerlessness, none of the tactics will work until you can shift your mindset and feel a little more personal control. So first you'll learn how to regain your personal power, if you need to, so you can then attack the challenge that led you to feel powerless in the first place.

In the sections on change, chaos, conflict, rejection, and illness or injury, you will learn more about what your brain and your emotions are experiencing as you go through each of those struggles, and you'll learn which resilience techniques are best suited for each one. The more techniques you know and can use to manage your struggles, the more flexible you can be. Reading this book, you won't just learn exactly which tactics match with which struggle, you'll also hopefully learn some new tactics, because the bigger the toolbox you have, the more flexible you can be when you need to overcome a stressful situation.

Each section also contains a Leader's Toolbox, with specific strategies for how to handle each state of struggle within a workplace setting. When an employee struggles, often an entire division or business struggles, and company leadership can be called upon to help navigate the effort. The techniques in the Leader's Toolbox section are intended to help you manage your employees in a fair and productive way.

LET'S FACE IT...WHEN YOU'RE STRUGGLING, NO MATTER WHAT the root cause, you just feel bad! But you don't have to stay stuck in that place, because there's a science behind feeling better, and we're going to unlock it with specific techniques designed to get right to the heart of your particular struggle. You're going to learn how to avoid wasting time trying techniques that aren't an appropriate fit for your problem, or tactics that would work for someone else but not you.

Every suggestion in the following chapters has been proven to work, and to work in specific ways, on specific problems. By the end of the book, you'll have assembled a toolbox full of tools you can use on any problem that challenges you. Knowing the right techniques will help you build resilience faster, and waste less time trying to cope in ways that don't work. Are you ready to stop struggling?

RECLAIMING POWER AND CONTROL

JACK WAS TRAILING HIS FINGERS ALONG THE DUST LEFT FROM when the World Trade Center had fallen two months earlier. He stood under the dusty scaffolding in ravaged lower Manhattan and turned me to with anguish on his face. "Man, we don't deserve this. This is awful. What are we going to do now?"

Jack and I had both just gotten the news: the company we were working for couldn't afford to keep us anymore, and Friday would be our last day. We stood on the street in front of our office building, processing what had just happened. He clenched his jaw, and I thought about the girlfriend he was making plans to propose to. The new apartment he had just moved in to.

With as much sales experience as he had, Jack would otherwise have been in hot demand. Jack had never had trouble finding a job before, but now the world was different. Ten weeks ago, Jack and I had stood in the street with our colleagues and watched the second plane hit the World Trade Center. We saw the towers begin to crumble. As the streets of lower Manhattan started to fill with people around us, we rushed back to the office to grab our belongings and head north, away from the chaos.

There was still a fine coating of dust all over New York a month later, when we first realized the business we worked for was in trouble. The company created the kind of fun, irreverent advertising that felt inappropriate in the wake of the September 11th attacks. One by one, our clients started to pull back the money they spent with us, or drop off completely. The first two people had been let go last week. Today, it was our turn.

But it wasn't just the job. Or the humiliation of being fired. I was looking at a young man who, for the first time in his life, had absolutely no idea what to do next. The world was in turmoil everywhere we turned. People were moving out, businesses were closing, the natural rhythm of the city was gone. As we stood there that September day and watched it happen, we had been unable to do anything to help. One of my colleagues had offered her cell phone to a crying woman— that was the extent of what we were able to do to assist. The world had gone from predictable to chaotic in a single fall morning.

Jack wondered how he could ever propose to his girlfriend after this—it wasn't just that he felt silly spending a fortune on a ring. But how could he look her in the eyes and promise her forever when people had died all around them? How do you commit to a lifetime when that promise is out of your control?

THE ORIGINAL ROOT CAUSE OF YOUR STRUGGLE MIGHT HAVE been change, or conflict, or chaos. It might have been a health challenge or a rejection. But if you grapple with any of those struggles for too long, you might have to address our your powerlessness, first. If you find yourself saying things like, "Nothing will ever change," or "It doesn't matter what I do," those are signs you've found yourself in a state of powerlessness. Start with this chapter and regain your belief in your control, before you flip to the other chapters.

What Jack was experiencing in that moment is common when we feel that we have lost control. Loss of control might feel like a struggle you can't overcome. After all, if you have no power, what can you do? How can you make an impact on the situation, or change anything? When we allow ourselves to believe we are powerless over a situation, we give up any chance of ever feeling better than we do today. We are, in essence, condemning ourselves to a world we dislike, because we have given up hope for a better future.

In this section, you will learn how to use both problem-focused and emotion-focused coping to regain your sense of control over your life and struggles. You will discover ways to correctly deploy three strategies research shows are most successful at helping you regain your lost power.

This section of the book is a little like triage: if you have slipped into powerlessness, then none of the other strategies in the book are going to be able to help you. A sense of powerlessness can actually be borne out of any of the other struggles in this book. When we fail to overcome those struggles, we run the risk of believing we are helpless to move beyond them. Over time, we slip into a feeling of powerlessness.

When you are feeling powerless, be aware that it may be difficult to even begin thinking about applying some of these strategies. When life feels out of your control, feeling powerless to change it can become a habit. But it doesn't have to be a habit from here on out, if you are willing to take a risk and try these research-proven strategies.

Why We Crave Control and What Happens When We Don't Get It

Losing control is frustrating because it is a threat to our autonomy. Much of our success in this world depends on being able to go out and "do" for ourselves. As we grow from childhood to adulthood, we set out to become more and more independent. Although we once relied on our parents and others around us to help us eat, sleep, and cross the street, the purpose of growing up is to wean away from that helplessness and forge our own path. Just like a toddler grabbing the spoonful of carrots from her mother, we're driven to stop being powerless and do it ourselves.

But there are points in everyone's life where our choices are taken away, and we become powerless once again. Powerlessness takes us back to our infancy, and our autonomy is threatened. What follows that threat to our autonomy is hopelessness. If we are unable to do what needs to be done, what good are we? How will we ever achieve our goals? While these hopeless thoughts may seem extreme, like they must only happen to people who experience severe depression, they aren't. In fact, in one study, 39% of college students experienced hopelessness during their years at university. When we fail to exert control over our environment, we grieve that lost power.

We also get frustrated at situations where we are powerless because we cannot predict the outcome. David Rock's SCARF model is one way of understanding social rewards and threats, and the model offers us some clues to what this powerlessness can feel like. Rock suggests that certainty plays a key role in our mental well-being, and the more we can predict what is likely to happen in the future, the more safe we feel. Without power, we lose the ability to both control and therefore predict what is going to happen to us. We feel at the mercy of the fates, or God, or whoever is the boss of us in any given moment.

The outcome of these experiences is a loss of motivation. When we feel helpless to affect the outcome, we are unmotivated to keep trying. Why would we want to bang our heads against the wall anymore? Often, uncontrollable situations ultimately cause us to lose our motivation. But when we lose our motivation, we have succumbed to the lowest stage of powerlessness: giving up.

Coming back from giving up isn't easy. The very nature of powerlessness whispers in your ear, "Don't even bother. There's nothing you can do." But research shows there **is** something you can do. When you have reached a state of hopelessness, it is important to use many tools in your toolbox at the same time, in order to regain your power and control.

To face down powerlessness, research shows it is essential to combine emotion-focused coping strategies with problem-focused coping strategies. Even though you may have a preference for one over the other, you'll need to use both types of strategies in order to fight the oversized monster that is hopelessness. Some research on coping strategies suggests that emotion-focused coping is less effective than problem-focused coping. After all, wouldn't it be better to fix the problem than just deal with the emotional fallout from it? But particularly in the area of powerlessness, the problem can't always **be** fixed, or fixed completely. When dealing with a powerless situation, therefore, it's best to use both problem-focused coping and emotion-focused coping, simultaneously. Doing both at the same time is proven to yield a better outcome.

One interesting thing to note about combining problem-focused coping and emotion-focused coping: studies show that perceived control, the amount of control you believe you have over a situation, is equally as important as actual control. So feeling like you have some control over a situation gives you the same benefit as if you actually had control. The **feeling** of control over something can be just as important as actual, tactical control, which means that when it comes to powerlessness, both emotions and tactics will play a role in overcoming the struggle.

When you are feeling powerless, combine two tactics to restabilize both your tactical control and your emotional control. Using both techniques simultaneously ups your ability to regain your sense of mastery and control over your environment, even if things seem out of your hands.

Strategy: Focus on What You Can Control

Back when I worked in sales, I sat in a cube farm full of other salespeople. Everyone could hear everyone else's phone conversations, so we all knew about every success and every failure our colleagues experienced. To my right was Abby, and to my left was Gus. Both were experienced and energetic salespeople, and I sometimes listened in to their calls, hoping to learn how to be good at sales.

Abby kept a list by her desk. She took copious notes of every sales call, and what the prospective clients had said about what they might be interested in buying. If they weren't interested, she still took notes. She wanted to know every detail of why they weren't going to buy from her. I once asked her why she took as many notes from a "no" customer as she did from a "yes" customer, because it seemed unusual. She told me, "If I know what they don't like, I know what needs to change. Maybe it's just the timing or the circumstance, but if it's something I can control, I'll fix it and make the sale."

Gus did things differently. He listened intently on calls, but when prospective clients weren't interested in talking to him, he was all too eager to get off the call. When I asked him once why a client he thought was going to buy didn't buy, he responded, "Eh, they just made a stupid decision. There was nothing I could have done to change their minds." Gus told himself he wasn't at fault for losing the sale, because the outcome was out of his control. Abby, on the other hand, gathered as much information as she could, because she believed that with the right information, she might be able to control the outcome.

People who successfully navigate a loss of control have been found to have an internal locus of control. An internal locus of control means that an individual feels he has impact over the things that occur in his life. Someone with an external locus of control, on the other hand, feels that the things that happen to him are outside of his control—that they are controlled by fate, luck, or are someone else's fault.

You might think that all situations in which we feel powerless render us helpless, and feeling like we have no control. But studies show that even in a powerless state, many people are still able to respond with an internal locus of control, and those people fare better in the long term.

Start by evaluating your own locus of control. Are you telling yourself that what happens is completely out of your hands? Does it feel like the fates are just against you, conspiring to make life terrible for you right now?

If that's how you feel, then you might be experiencing an external locus of control, and you'll feel a noticeable upswing in how powerful you feel if you start to shift it. To make the shift, use the two-pronged approach of both problem-focused and emotion-focused tactics. On the problem-focused side, perhaps this is where you try a new solution to the problem, something completely out of the box that you haven't tried before. One last-ditch effort aimed at out-of-the-box thinking is worth it. In fact, some of the most creative problem-solvers have stumbled across breakthrough ideas when they were just about to give up.

When it comes to shifting your locus of control from an emotion-focused stance, behaviors like meditation can be a huge benefit. In the first place, meditation helps you find calmness, but more importantly, when you take on a new behavior like meditation, you are also exercising control over your own life. Finding power in the small things is a step on the path to feeling more emotionally in control.

Shifting your focus incorporates both the tactical and the emotional techniques, because you are emotionally letting go of trying to control the original problem, while simultaneously taking up a new task over which you have more control. Find something in life that you enjoy and have a sense of mastery over. Perhaps a new hobby, a new project at work, something you can do with friends and family. Maybe it was something you have been doing all along, but you haven't been paying attention to it since the feelings of powerlessness came along.

As you practice focus-shifting, remember: perceived control is just as important as actual control. If you had obvious control, it's likely you wouldn't be feeling powerless in the first place, so try to take this suggestion to heart, and find some place in your life where you can exercise control and power. Shifting your focus to something you can control is like a double-whammy solution: It provides a level of emotional distraction and soothing, **and** it employs problem-solving tactics on something you have influence over.

What techniques can you use to exert your influence on the things you can control?

1. **Find a coach.** Coaching is a valuable problem-focused technique. The coaching could be either within the workplace, like a mentor, or could be an outside professional. Obtaining outside coaching is a great way to uncover areas of your life and work that are within your control, and it's a positive, action-oriented step you can take that doesn't require a lot of preparatory time or energy, which you might feel drained of in a powerless situation.

2. **Make a list.** Start writing down your past accomplishments. Dig as far back as you can to find moments where you shone. Go further than your résumé, to find the things that highlight your skills and talents. This list is a great reflection tool, showing you

exactly when and where you were at your most powerful, and illuminating those times when you had the most control. It also serves as a reminder that there have been moments of great success and personal power in your life, even if you don't feel that way right now. The list doesn't just have to be professional accomplishments, either—list times when you were a great parent, partner, child, or friend.

3. **Get a new view.** Analyze the situation from a different angle, perhaps getting input from someone else. When you are feeling powerless, you are likely also feeling blocked. This prevents you from coming up with solutions. Have you ever heard a friend's story and thought, "I know exactly what I'd do in that situation. I don't know why they can't just…?" If so, then you know how easy it can be to solve someone **else's** problem. But it often isn't easy to solve our own. A great application of problem-focused coping is to step outside of the situation and use a new viewpoint to see your way out of whatever situation feels unsolvable and hopeless.

Strategy: Change the Story You Tell Yourself

Another element of powerlessness that has proven to be important is explanatory style. Explanatory style is the story we tell ourselves about why things happen to us. Just as locus of control is a way to tell ourselves who is responsible for the things that happen to us, explanatory style is a way to describe **why** these things are happening.

Explanatory style (also known by some as "attributional style") has three elements: personal, permanent, and pervasive. If someone is using a negative explanatory style, it might show up as thinking that the things that happen to her are personal. Perhaps you know someone who assumes that if you don't return her phone call immediately, you no longer like her. She's making an assumption

LEADER'S
Toolbox

Helping Your Employees
Empower Themselves

AS A LEADER IN YOUR WORKPLACE, YOU MAY COME ACROSS powerlessness among your employees. As we discussed, powerlessness often stems from an inability to correctly manage some of the other struggle situations. Your team members may become powerless after a major change, conflict in the workplace, or if they are overwhelmed. They might also exhibit powerlessness as a result of personal issues at home.

When your employees are in a state of powerlessness, they aren't able to do their best work. There are things you can do as a manager to help your team members avoid feelings of hopelessness and regain their control. In these situations, you will want to provide both problem-focused strategies and emotion-focused strategies, to be sure that they cope in the best possible way.

Problem-focused coping opportunities you can provide as a manager might be:

- Informational meetings, where they can have a greater understanding of all the issues that might be causing them to feel stuck.

- Workplace coaching opportunities, so that they have a mentor with whom to work through solutions.

- Help with goal setting, in order to give them a positive place to focus their efforts.

Emotion-focused coping opportunities you can provide as a manager might look like:

- Team volunteering efforts, where they can find perspective and regain their power by helping others.

- Chances for mental health breaks during the day or week, like group yoga or 3-minute Avanoo training sessions (*www.Avanoo.com*).

that everything is personal! Of course, the real reason you didn't call her back has nothing to do with her. You have a deadline at work, a sick child, or a volunteer commitment ran long. It isn't personal, but she interprets that it **must** be personal, because she is assigning a negative explanation to things that happen to her.

Another element of explanatory style is pervasiveness. A person who finds negative explanations for things in life might believe that the difficult things going on in one environment are seeping over into all the other areas of life. A person like this might assume that because something went wrong at home that morning, his entire day is going to be a disaster. And once he makes that assumption, he's somehow usually proven correct by having a terrible rest of the day!

The final element of negative explanatory style is permanence. If someone is using a negative explanatory style, she feels like whatever is going wrong now will go wrong forever. A person using a negative explanatory style might say that whatever is going wrong now cannot ever be fixed, no matter what.

I knew a woman once who lost all belief in her ability to succeed, and she felt it would never come back. Lina and I were both about to graduate from college right after the burst of the dot com bubble. She, like many of our fellow students, had been offered an amazing job that she had been counting on, but Lina's offer was pulled a month before graduation. The company could no longer afford to hire her.

She applied for a backup job—she wasn't thrilled about it the way she was about her first job, but it was still a good option. The day the rejection letter from the backup job arrived in the mail, Lina was despondent. She didn't qualify for the position, and they were looking for someone with more experience.

"I didn't get the job. I'm not smart enough to work there," she lamented. "I just don't have what they're looking for."

Lina didn't have what they were looking for **right then**, but her rejection was simply because of a lack of time in the field, not a question of her overall intelligence. Lina, however, had adopted a negative explanatory style. She was telling herself that she didn't get the job because she wasn't smart enough. She perceived intellect as a more or less permanent trait, so in telling herself the story that she didn't get the job because of an innate quality, she was making the explanation permanent.

The real explanation why Lina didn't get the job is that she needed more experience, which is a factor she **could** change. Explanatory style is a powerful thing—it can have us believe things that aren't true about our lives and why things happen to us. And when it comes to powerlessness, telling ourselves that something is permanent is one of the most destructive things we can do. If your explanatory style needs a shift, take a hard look at permanence, specifically, because that's where a lot of powerlessness stems from.

Once powerlessness has developed, we're at great risk for something known as "learned helplessness." Learned helplessness is an outcome of telling ourselves that the state of powerless is permanent. After all, once you've banged your head into a wall for the 10th time, there isn't much more you can do, is there? When researchers tried to replicate learned helplessness in the lab, they started with dogs. They separated the dogs into three groups. The first group of dogs was administered a small shock, but also provided a way to escape the shock by jumping over a barrier. The second group of dogs was also administered the shock, but were given no way to escape. The third group of dogs, the control group, had nothing done to them in round one.

In round two, all three groups of dogs were administered the shock and provided a way to escape. The first group of dogs, who had learned to escape the shocks before, figured out how to escape the shocks again. The control group of dogs, who hadn't experienced any shocks before, also learned how to escape the shocks. But the second group of dogs, who earlier had been unable to find any relief from the shock, didn't even try to find an escape this time. They just lay down and whimpered until the experiment ended. Even though an escape was available, they didn't bother to look. They had learned to give up.

When a situation lasts a long time with no relief, we are at risk of learning to be helpless. Those feelings of powerlessness can grow until we want to give up, like the dogs. Powerlessness lies to us and makes us feel that, because we have no control, this situation might go on forever, and we might always feel this way.

In order to overcome powerlessness, then, we must change the story we are telling ourselves. This struggle is not permanent. It will not last forever. And we are not helpless as we fight through it.

What techniques work to help you change the story you're telling yourself?

1. **Journal your thoughts and experiences.** Expressive writing has been shown to improve mood and happiness levels. Journaling even five minutes a day gives you a way to put your beliefs down on paper and revisit them at a later time. When you look back over what you've written, look for your explanatory style. Are you assuming things will be permanent? Once you put something in writing, it is easier to evaluate it for what is true and what negative beliefs you might be holding on to. You can also write about times in your life when you succeeded, as a way to remind your brain that the struggle you are facing now hasn't always existed, and won't, in fact, be permanent.

2. **Talk about it.** Have conversations with loved ones, both about your struggle and about theirs. When we talk honestly with our friends and family members, and have to put into words what we're experiencing, we're likely to get some perspective and support. Perhaps we aren't the only ones facing a catastrophic struggle, and talking about it to other people means we open our eyes to the struggles of others.

3. **Find some om.** Try meditation or yoga, both of which help your mental well-being. Whether you want to refocus your mind on the task at hand or distract your mind from struggling, these two techniques give you the brain-break you can use to interrupt what feels like a hopeless downward spiral.

Strategy: Rebuild Your Motivation

Have you begun to believe that this period of helplessness is going to last forever? Does this feel like a pit of despair from which you'll never be able to crawl out? Perhaps you feel like you'll never reach your goal, whether it's life-related, work-related, or anything else. Studies show that when we feel powerless, we naturally lose our motivation. Resilience strategies to address powerlessness, therefore, must not only just make us **feel** better, but must also rekindle our lost motivation.

Carrie emailed me after a presentation I gave for an association in her industry. Her father and mother had owned the family business for years, and Carrie worked for them as a manager, but the business was going under as more and more of their customers shopped online. Not only was the business struggling, but her father and mother were going to lose their house in the next few months, if things kept going on the same trajectory. They had focused all of their energy and money on keeping the business, but Carrie knew if they lost the house, it would be disastrous.

At the same time she was worried about her parents' future, Carrie also knew if the business folded she herself would be out of work. She had her parents' blessing to start the job hunt, but she just couldn't bring herself to send out her résumé.

When the struggle seems too steep to overcome, and we feel too powerless to begin the fight, like Carrie did, we've lost our motivation. We have to get it back, because without it, there's no gas in our tank for the road ahead.

What techniques are the most successful at rebuilding your motivation?

1. **Re-set your goals.** One of the key techniques to rebuild your motivation is by refocusing on our goals. When we refocus on our goals, or revise our goals to make new ones, we're taking active steps toward our future, and that automatically reduces our powerlessness. In fact, re-setting your goals manages to be both a problem-focused **and** emotion-focused strategy, all wrapped up in one! Goal setting itself is a tactical, problem-ori-

ented technique, but focusing on the future is also an optimistic way of looking at the future, and stoking the fires of optimism is good for your emotions, too!

Perhaps you have some past goals hanging over your head, taunting you because you never reached them. We often think that we are supposed to set goals and never stray from them no matter what. We might have been told that abandoning our goals is giving up, so we cling to them because we don't want to be a quitter, even though we feel powerless. But goals that no longer serve you are just millstones around your neck. They can act as bitter reminders during a time when you need to be focusing on what is possible. Let go of goals that are no longer relevant or serving a purpose. You can always reinstate them later if the time is right. In the meantime, refocus on goals that are within your grasp. Working toward them and accomplishing them will give you a tremendous boost of personal power.

2. **Try something new.** Another technique to try is picking up a hobby or activity outside the environment in which you are struggling. Often a feeling of powerlessness can be tied to a certain environment in our lives. When we get outside of that environment, it's easier to take risks and feel accomplished. Trying something new can be a great way to re-develop a sense of autonomy, and it gives you a new area of life where you can set and achieve goals. Is there a sport or an art you wish you had mastered, but never did? Adding a new joy to your life is a great way to find fresh motivation.

3. **Volunteer.** In my book, *The Giving Prescription*, volunteering was the number one way that people going through serious life traumas could regain their power. Interestingly, it wasn't a matter of feeling sorry for someone who has it worse than you. Instead, volunteering worked to help people get motivated

because they were able to recognize that no matter how badly they were struggling, they still had the power to affect someone's life in a positive way.

A Final Thought On Taking Back Your Power

No matter how powerless you feel, your life is not completely out of your grasp. Deploying the two-pronged method of both tactics and emotions has you sidestepping helplessness and lifting yourself to a place of personal power once again.

To focus on what you can control, try:

• Getting a coach

• Listing your past accomplishments

• Looking at situations from a new perspective

To change the story you tell yourself, try:

• Journaling

• Having honest conversations

• Meditating

To rebuild your motivation, try:

• Refocusing on past goals

• Picking up a new hobby

• Volunteering

NAVIGATING CHANGE

GABE BARELY RECOGNIZED HIMSELF. EVER SINCE THE BABY WAS born, he was like a different person. He dreaded his commute home, because he knew when he walked through the door he would start to feel annoyed. The house always felt messy, and the baby fussed from colic. No matter how hard he tried, he could barely keep himself from snapping at Amy, his wife. Everything she said seemed to Gabe like a criticism of him, of his failures to make their life perfect.

At work, Gabe found himself struggling to get excited about his new project. The clients seemed exciting enough, but starting a new project was the last thing Gabe wanted to be doing right now. No matter how hard he tried, he seemed to have lost his creativity and just couldn't produce the same caliber of work he used to. Not to mention he really needed to excel on this project, because the new boss had taken over three weeks earlier, and had his eye on Gabe for a possible promotion. If Gabe didn't impress the new guy, his chances of moving up in the company were dismal.

Even when Gabe got away from all the stressors of work and home, he just didn't feel right. Mark, his best friend, had just gotten married and decided to skip their annual guys' trip to the beach that summer. Gabe could really have used the long weekend away, but Mark didn't think he could pull it off so close after the wedding. Gabe could feel Mark pulling away, and he understood, but he really needed his buddy around.

And when he held his new baby daughter in his hands, Gabe was happy but concerned. How was he going to afford to pay for everything she needed? How was he going to make money at work when he could barely focus from the lack of sleep he was getting?

He remembered how much he couldn't wait for her to be born—how he used to talk to her when she was still just a bump in Amy's belly. He had been so excited to meet her, and had made all sorts of plans for what kind of father he would be. But now that she was here, everything was different. She and Amy needed him 24/7, and he wasn't used to the pressure. He wasn't sure he could even handle it. He knew he had signed on to be a father, but he didn't know it was going to be like this.

So when the dishwasher broke in the middle of the seventh cycle of bottle parts that week, Gabe lost it. He slammed his hands on the marble countertop and yelled at Amy: "Seriously? I can't TAKE this anymore! I HATE THIS!" Amy ran out of the room with her face in her hands.

Gave obviously didn't hate the dishwasher, Amy, the baby, or really anything else about his life. He just hated the dramatic changes happening on all fronts.

ONE OF THE MAIN REASONS CHANGE IS UNWELCOME IS BECAUSE it destabilizes us. We work so hard to make our lives stable and secure, then change comes along and knocks us off our old course, and on to a new.

Many times when we are faced with change, we have a hard time shifting our focus off of the old course we feel forced to abandon. We have a tendency to cling to that old path we feel we are "supposed" to be on. Or perhaps we focus on the confusion of feeling off-course and adrift. The challenge of navigating change comes from handling these feelings enough to let go of them and shift our concentration toward the new path ahead. If we don't find a way to navigate through change, we're at risk for losing our place in a changing environment. Without the ability to change alongside the environment, we will be labeled rigid and left behind.

On your first day of school, you were excited and scared. You didn't know if your teacher would be mean or nice. You wondered if the other students would like you. You weren't sure where you were supposed to eat lunch, or which desk was yours, or why you had to raise your hand to ask a question. Starting school might have been one of the biggest changes in your life thus far. And yet by high school, being a student has become a routine. What was once an intimidating transition became a way of life. And so it is with most of life's changes.

Change can knock us off balance, damage our self-esteem, and leave us questioning our place in the world. But it doesn't have to be that way. Well-executed change brings us closer to our goals, a fact for which we will ultimately be grateful, even if the process of getting there is painful. The way we manage change has everything to do with how successful the change ends up being.

In this chapter I'll offer strategies that research has shown can help you connect with purpose in the midst of change, stay engaged when you feel like withdrawing, and maintain a sense of self-belief as the world around you is shifting. You may never be immune from the discomfort of evolution, but you won't feel so adrift when you are faced with life's one constant: change.

Change Knocks Us Off Balance

Change has a tendency to make the ground beneath us seem less firm. We might have known where to stand and what to do five minutes ago, but now we're not so sure.

Whether the changes we face are at work or at home, we can do three things to ease the transition:

- **Communicate**—freely get and give information. Don't shut down or close off
- **Find social support**—seek supervision and supportive networks
- **Build self-belief**—focus on the things you can control, and build your confidence in your abilities

These three smaller tactics all play a role in building engagement, the overarching technique that helps you navigate change. When you are able to do those three things successfully, you will have the ability to embrace transitions in life and in work. You will feel more flexible when life throws you a curveball you weren't expecting. You will be able to explain the benefits of growth and change to others, as a leader.

According to Dan and Chip Heath, the authors of *Switch: How to Change When Change is Hard*, one of the things that makes change so difficult to wrap our minds around is that it involves both the head and the heart. Because our heads and our hearts are motivated in two different ways, it can be difficult to get the needs of the two aligned.

In fact, the Heath brothers tell us that so often we try to "solve the problem" of change by using our heads, which only leads us to further confusion during the time of change. When we get in a problem-solving mindset, we tend to focus on the things that are struggling the most. That makes sense, they tell us, if most things are going smoothly. Give the squeaky wheel the grease, right? But in times of change, if we spend all our focus on the problem areas, we are likely to burn out. Instead, the Heaths' research suggests we start by looking at what is going right, and build on the things that are working. In times of change, it is better to walk toward something positive than away from something negative.

Change doesn't set out to be the enemy, although it can often be draining when it occurs, both in the professional sphere and in our personal lives. When managed poorly, change is frustrating, exhausting, and scary. When managed properly, change is helpful, cathartic, and usually necessary.

Change can be either transactional or relational. Transactional change involves very little emotion, and relies on a simple change in circumstance. Relational change shifts the world, its meaning, and our place in it. Transactional change doesn't usually require a struggle to get through, and in fact often goes unnoticed. But all too often, change means evolving our relationship to people or the world, and that's when it gets tricky.

We often decide whether change is going to be good for us or bad for us before we've even gotten very far into the process. Perhaps we base our evaluation on whether or not we chose the change, or feel it was forced upon us. Perhaps we judge change because it interrupts a status quo we're enjoying, or that we worked hard to achieve.

Change has a tendency to separate us from our surroundings. We become adrift when the familiarity goes missing, and both our head and our heart feel the discomfort of transformation. When we are struggling to navigate change, the more we can engage with our environment, the more likely it will be that we can triumph over the change.

Strategy: Connect With the Purpose, Not the Struggle

Laura was still living out of a suitcase eight weeks after her move. She had unpacked all of her son's things, but hadn't yet found time to organize her own, so every day she rifled through boxes to find something that didn't clash terribly before heading in to the kitchen to make pancakes. Pancakes were her son's favorite, and she worried the move had been hard on him, so she had been making his favorite foods every day for weeks to try to provide him a sense of normalcy.

But no one was making sure the move was easy on Laura. Every day felt like a struggle. She hadn't yet discovered the fastest route to work. She hadn't found the best dry cleaner or drug store. She didn't know which Chinese places delivered, for those nights she had to stay at the office late. Everything felt so much more difficult than it had been back home.

Laura came up to me at an event where I was speaking. She asked what she could do to manage how lost and discouraged she felt because of the move. "Well, why is it that you feel discouraged?" I asked her. "Discouraged means you feel let down. Why do you feel let down?"

"I just thought the move was going to make things easier," she said. "I wanted to move so my son and I could be closer to my parents. I'm a single mom, so having them nearby will be helpful, plus he'll have a better relationship with them." When she told me it had only been eight weeks, she looked up with surprise on her face, and didn't even wait for me to say anything before she answered herself. "It **has** only been eight weeks, I guess. Maybe it will get easier, just not yet?"

Laura moved to make life easier, but when life didn't become easy right away, she forgot the greater purpose of the move. She had made a well-thought-out decision to be closer to her parents, but felt frustrated when the change didn't immediately solve her problems. Change is like that—the long-term outcome is often worth it, but the path to get there is rocky.

One way to enjoy immediate relief from the discomfort of change is to recognize that change is a discrete event. Change doesn't last forever. Research shows recognizing that change isn't permanent helps people cope with the immediate struggle, by realizing that there is an end in sight. This recognition that the struggle will be over at some point gives you an emotional boost not only because you can see the light at the end of the tunnel, but also because you come to realize that change will not, in fact, take over your whole world. Focusing on the eventual ending can minimize the scary, all-consuming feeling change can bring.

Once you have accepted that the change won't last forever, research says the most important step you can take is to re-engage with the root issue or environment where the change is occurring. Change often makes people feel burned-out; in fact, change fatigue happens to most of us if we go through more changes than we feel like we can handle without a break. However, when we feel change fatigue or burned out we're likely to disengage from our environment, and that doesn't bode well for our ability to manage the change.

Burned-out individuals can re-engage by seeing the change in a new light. In *The Way of Transition*, author William Bridges believes there is a difference between change and transition. All too often, he writes, we get caught up in the moment of change, and forget about the transition that occurs afterward, as we get used to the change. In his mind, the transition that comes after the moment of change is most important.

Recognizing that change has a meaning, a purpose, has been found to be helpful in re-engaging after a big change. In fact, making meaning out of change appears to make the change not only easier to swallow, but often leads to appreciation of the change, after the fact. One of the best ways to come to grips with change appears to be finding some greater purpose for how your work, relationships, or life will be left following the change, as Laura did.

With that in mind, perhaps you can take your mind off the change for a while, and instead look at where the path of change is headed.

All transition has a purpose, as a path that is going somewhere else. If you can get engaged with where the path is **going**, it might allow you to **dis**engage emotionally from the struggle of the change.

Explanatory style, which we talked about in the previous chapter, can also help us as we challenge ourselves to look for the purpose behind a change. Big changes are a time in life when we have a tendency to throw up our hands and ask, "Why is this happening to me?" When we behave that way, however, we're making the change personal. We're acting like we're the only one who ever had to deal with change, or as though the mere presence of change is a personal affront to us.

If you catch yourself taking change too personally, then you're focusing on the wrong thing. You are likely focusing on the pain of the change, and not the greater purpose behind the change. What good things will the change bring? What struggles will the change address or fix? What opportunities will come about as a result of this change? When we shift our focus to the possibilities that can arise from the change, instead of taking it personally, we're more likely to be able to handle change with grace.

What techniques help you connect to the purpose behind the change, instead of the struggle of change?

1. **Journal about the future.** Start projecting forward to life following the upheaval of change. As you write about what life will be like after the change, you are reminding yourself that this change will one day be over, and imagining possibilities for the future. For many people, it can help to skip several years out, or else you can risk getting caught up in journaling about the current state of change. But skipping past the struggle, well into the future, allows your logical mind to rest, and your creative, problem-solving mind to see an enjoyable future. Once you have a positive vision for the future, you can work backward from there and reverse engineer what it will take to get there.

2. **List your opportunities.** Change brings plenty of struggle, but it also brings opportunities. Make a list of all the opportunities this current change might provide. Start with the most obvious, but spend enough time on the list that you stretch even to some unlikely possibilities. Being forced down a new and uncomfortable path is the typical beginning to many a hero story with a happy ending. Your change is likely to have terrific outcomes, and when you begin to grapple with change by listing the opportunities to come, it becomes easier to handle.

3. **Make change less personal.** Work on shifting your explanatory style so that you aren't describing the change in a way that is personal. Listen to the voice in your head: can you catch yourself describing the change as an individual insult? If so, you are taking the change personally. As you talk to friends and family members, are you telling stories about how the change is painful for **you**? Every time you catch yourself talking about your personal struggle with the change, offset that story by reminding yourself that the change is bigger than you, and is happening for reasons besides just you.

Strategy: Stay Engaged

During my time as a nonprofit founder and executive director, I took several courses in leadership and nonprofit management. One of my fellow classmates, David, a program development officer, found himself at a crossroads during the time we were in class together. The board of his nonprofit had just completed a strategic plan that included a complete overhaul of the direction of some of the organization's longtime programs. As a result of the changes, David's day-to-day work would be evolving to be more centered in a different area.

David struggled with the new direction called for by the overhaul, and particularly by the direct impact the changes would have

LEADER'S
Toolbox

Leading Through Change

MUCH RESEARCH HAS BEEN DONE ON ORGANIZATIONAL change in the workplace, and how management can better implement change to reduce staff turnover and keep organizational commitment high. Among the most successful tactics for corporate change management are communication, asking employees for input, and sharing decision-making and control. When a company deploys these techniques to help reduce the strain of change, employee satisfaction can remain consistent, even in the face of large-scale or ongoing change.

Good Business Change Tactic #1 is communication. Businesses who want to make change easier to navigate will give their employees plenty of information, and allow them safe spaces to communicate with both their peers and their managers about the changes. They will answer employees' questions, and let their voices be heard.

When researchers studied companies that successfully navigate workplace change, they found the businesses had several things in common. First, the companies excelled at communicating. They communicated not only the details of the change, but also the purpose behind the change. When constituents (employees, clients, leadership, etc.) understand the meaning of a change and the new direction, they are more likely to get on board with the change. But this acceptance can only come with a great deal of information. Companies who practice regular communication with their employees through a change are much more likely to have buy-in at all levels, and successfully navigate change.

Good Business Change Tactic #2 is asking for input. Businesses going through change should seek input and advice from every level of the company, both high and low. Organizations who were found to successfully navigate change found ways to turn the communication tables around and ask for input. During large changes, it might seem overwhelming to get too much input, but communication going from the bottom up, and not just the top down, is also a critical factor in making change work at a company level.

Finally, Good Business Change Tactic #3 is sharing control and decision-making. On an individual level, change can be a time when we feel a distinct loss of control, so anything that helps us regain that control will provide comfort. As you know from the previous chapter on powerlessness and loss of control, employees who feel powerless will be less able to contribute to a successful business.

Organizations who use two-way communications as a way to share control and share decision-making are better at navigating organizational change. During a period of change, it's common for participants to feel helpless, particularly if they were not involved in initiating the change. By sharing decision-making powers during the change, organizations were able to measurably increase employee commitment and satisfaction.

Change can make even the most capable of organizations lose their footing. As such, change needs to be thought of as a tool that can be either dangerous or helpful, depending on how it is used. To use it wisely requires just a little bit of knowledge. One worldwide travel company provides a great example: their marketplace is online, yet in the ever-changing Internet world, they have easily evolved to keep up, every step of the way.

This travel company has grown exponentially since its initial public offering, acquiring several companies and integrating those new companies into the original brand. Change was frequent for several years, and during this rapid growth and acquisition phase, managers at the company communicated faithfully with staff both new and existing. They held frequent meetings to talk about the parameters of the change, and let employees know what they could expect in the coming weeks and months.

One leader at the company credits the success of their acquisitions to early visits. Instead of doing what many large organizations do, and sending senior staff to the new office, this organization takes the extra step of flying new employees to **their** headquarters. Why? To show these employees what they are now a part of. To put into context the reasons for the acquisition. To explain what the company's growth will mean to them.

Can you imagine having a new boss halfway across the globe? With new strategies and ideas and values? It happens at companies every day. By flipping the model on its head and inviting newly-acquired employees to come to **them,** the company sends an early message that this change is going to be different. This change is going to have their best interests at the center.

Leadership at this company also knows that communication is a key way that change is embraced at an organizational level. Having access to information makes a change go more smoothly for the organization. But remember, the research also suggests that what takes away the sting of change at a personal level is purpose and meaning. Leaders put change into context when they open the door to newly acquired employees, get them excited about the vision for the change, and give the change a meaning, a reason for existing. As another employee put it, "It was obvious we weren't cogs in the machine to them, but participants in the truly special business they are building." In communicating the purpose of the change, this company successfully navigates what can, for many organizations, be a thorny time.

Engagement is the number one tool that helps make change easier to swallow. Change involves us, therefore it must also **include us**. To conquer change, keep employees engaged with information and purpose.

on his role. First he noticed that he didn't speak up as much during staff meetings. His mom had told him that if he didn't have anything nice to say, then don't say anything at all. He didn't want to come across as negative, so he thought keeping quiet would be best. David soon found himself looking for excuses to get out of the office as much as he could, like scheduling meetings off-site.

By the time David told me about what was going on at work, he was disengaged, but he didn't even realize it. Somewhere along the line, he had just stopped investing as much of himself in his work.

Do you remember the one thing research shows is the critical piece to successfully navigating change? It's engagement. Staying engaged has been shown to be one of the best singular buffers to change. Whether with work, with your family, with your relationship—whatever the arena your change is happening in, it is important to stay engaged to the environment at hand if you want to successfully navigate your way through the transition.

When you go through a change, it is healthy to seek information and have conversations. There are two things you can do to accomplish this, in the wake of any change. First, communication is key. Don't shut down in the wake of change, be it personal or professional. Continue having conversations, seeking information. Whatever you do, don't keep it all inside. It's natural to pull into yourself during a change. Resist this tendency!

Along the same line, the second thing you can do to remain engaged is find social support. Social support has been found to be a stabilizing factor for people going through change, and helps people keep a consistent and level-headed view of themselves, even when the world is changing around them. Some research suggests that social support also helps reduce stress during times of change, because it helped people feel less out of control. When we give and receive support from other people during a time of change, we feel like we're actually participating in the process of change, which helps us embrace it. Seek out peers, mentors, or friends to provide you with the social support you need to stay engaged.

If you aren't able to get re-engaged in whatever arena of your life is changing, or if getting re-engaged isn't helping reduce the strain of the change, try to get engaged with something else. Become passionate about a new hobby, or anything where your energies can be directed at something fresh and exciting. The goal is to find a place to direct your passions that is stable and reliable while you work through the transition, and hopefully will keep you feeling positive and excited about something until the worst of the change has passed.

Using communication and social support, you can remain engaged in the change in a healthy way, without focusing on the feelings of fear and exhaustion that change can so often bring. When you build engagement, you offer yourself a way to play an active role in the change while at the same time creating a positive emotional relationship with the change. Engagement helps you both practically and psychologically confront the change head-on.

What techniques can you use to stay engaged in the face of change?

1. **Use your words.** Because of the uncertainty that accompanies change, we might feel inclined to sit back and watch before participating. Just as sailors wait and see which way the wind is blowing, we may have been taught to evaluate a situation before we say anything. But communication ranks at the top of the list for ways to stay engaged in your environment during a change. If you feel uncertain about how to communicate, start by asking questions. Clarify elements of the change that are confusing. Just be sure to avoid negative or draining communications, like venting, which we'll discuss more in the next chapter. When you communicate with others during a change, you are actually indicating you hold a position of strength (even if it doesn't feel like it!).

2. **Build a support network.** Change can be so mentally draining that we might just want to crawl into bed and pull the covers over our heads. But in order to stay engaged with the change, it helps to surround yourself with supportive people. Be honest when gathering a support network to you during a time of change: tell them, "I'm going through a great deal of transition

right now, and I could use your support. Do I have your permission to call you for support?" **For best results,** gather two groups on whom you can rely: one group who is connected to the environment where the change is occurring, and one group in a completely separate arena. With two types of supportive groups, you'll have feedback and reinforcement from two points of view, which can often be helpful when looking for advice or just a place to distract yourself and recharge.

Strategy: Regain Your Personal Power

When David, whose nonprofit was going in a new direction, recognized that he had lost his passion for his work, he knew he had to try to get it back. He wasn't sure, however, where he should start. Over a lunch break during our class one day, I asked him what had drawn him to work at the organization to begin with.

"I loved the feeling I would get when I went into the field to work with our clients. Being able to help them change their lives was amazing—it just felt so good to use my knowledge to help someone else. I always left feeling great," he told me.

"Well, if you want to feel that spark again, why don't you start with what worked before?" I asked him. "Why not spend some more time out in the field?"

Two weeks later I saw David again, and he had an energy coming off of him that I hadn't seen before.

"I did it!" he exclaimed. "I went back out to the field and it made me feel great. I helped two families in one day! I really do love this job, because I love the outcome of what we do."

What David experienced, when he went back and re-visited his favorite parts of the job, was finding the sweet spot of his personal power. He started doing what he did best and loved most, and it felt great. When we spend time focusing on our own abilities and accomplishments and drivers, we feel more capable of managing the change that comes our way.

The belief that you are capable is called "self-efficacy," and self-efficacy is a large predictor of how well you manage many of life's struggles, especially change. Self-efficacy is the source of a lot of our personal power: If you believe in yourself and your abilities, you'll be much more mentally prepared to navigate change. Studies show that self-belief is almost as helpful to navigating change as being one of the key decision-makers regarding the change in the first place!

Research on organizational change within companies highlights exactly why self-efficacy can be so critical to managing change. Jimmieson, Terry and Callan found that "employees who doubt their ability to respond to the demands of a specific organizational change are likely to focus attention on their feelings of incompetence, which will be accompanied by feelings of psychological distress and a failure to deal with the situation." To effectively adapt, it helps if you can work to control the tendency toward self-doubt.

It's interesting to note that self-efficacy can cross the boundaries of work and home; if you aren't feeling so powerful and competent at work, the things you do in your personal life can still build up your belief in yourself, and vice versa. Knowing this, you have lots of options for ways you can regain a feeling of power, all of which will translate to the environment where you are experiencing change.

What techniques work to regain your personal power?

1. **Get a hobby.** If you aren't feeling a lot of confidence in yourself lately, you might want to start looking outside of the environment where the change is taking place. What confidence-boosting activities can you be a part of? Are there hobbies where you excel? Finding a hobby where you can be successful is a great first step in reclaiming personal power. If you have ever felt "in the zone," you know how enjoyable it feels to try an activity where

you are putting in effort and focus, but not so much effort that the activity is no longer enjoyable. That feeling, first described by Mihaly Csikszentmihalyi, is called "flow state," and it can be great for your mental well-being. Look for a hobby where you find a state of flow. Try to take on a leadership role in that domain, and grow your belief in yourself.

2. **Make a contribution.** Once you have built some extra self-belief in an arena outside the environment that is changing, start to translate that power to your current stressful situation. Ask yourself: "How can I contribute to the current situation? What do I have to offer?" Research shows people who have self-confidence about their ability to navigate change take a more active role in the change. On top of that, people who take an active role in the change, instead of a passive role, are better able to cope with change. When you contribute to the change or take an active role in its management, you reinforce your personal power, and your feelings about the change actually become more positive.

A Final Thought On Navigating Change

Remember, change doesn't last forever. It's a snapshot in time on your way to somewhere else. Engaging with that change is the most effective vehicle that will get you from here to there in a timely fashion, with the least amount of upheaval.

Perhaps, as the popular song says, "a change will do you good."

To stay connected to the purpose of change, try:

- Journaling about what life will be like after the change
- Making a list of opportunities the change will bring
- Shifting your explanatory style so that the change feels less personal

To stay engaged despite the change, try:

- Communicating with those around you
- Finding social support of like-minded people

To regain your personal power, try:

- Finding an outside hobby where you feel accomplished and powerful
- Contributing to the changing environment in a meaningful way

CONTROLLING CHAOS

AMANDA'S DESK PHONE RANG FOR THE EIGHTH TIME THAT HOUR. It was her boss, with another question about the proposal he was putting together for the opening of the new location. Things had been crazy at work ever since they had signed the lease to take over and renovate a giant building in the next town. Amanda was pulling 12 hour days or longer. Being the point person on the new building would have been okay if Amanda hadn't had to do all her own work on top of it. Her boss didn't seem to notice that she was basically working two jobs.

The hardest part was that she kept having to switch from one job to the other, and it was driving her crazy to transition back and forth. She had suggested to her boss that perhaps she devote her mornings to her regular duties, and her afternoons to the new site project, but he rejected that idea. Questions might come up at any time of day, he replied, and she needed to be ready to answer them immediately. What that meant for Amanda was working five minutes on one thing, and five minutes on another, and she could barely get in the zone with anything before another email pinged onto her computer screen, demanding her attention and pulling her away from whatever work she was just starting to make headway on.

Then her phone rang for the ninth time. She picked it up, imagining her boss on the other end of the line as she answered. Certainly there was some permit that needed handling, or a contractor to check in with. But it wasn't him. Instead, it was the elementary school. Her daughter Chloe had thrown up during social studies, and was in the nurse's office. How soon could Amanda be there to pick her up?

Amanda looked at the pile of paperwork on her desk. She had hours more work to do today, and she couldn't take time off this afternoon to sit at home with a sick kid. But her husband Craig was away on a business trip, and there was no one else to do it. Chloe didn't want anybody but mommy when she was sick, anyway. Shoving a stack of files in her bag, Amanda called her boss on her cell phone and told him where she was going. She called the secretary and asked for her calls to be transferred to her cell phone for the rest of the day.

As she slid behind the wheel, she turned on the hands free phone connection in her car – thank God for that! – and dialed her son's best friend's mom. She offered to drive carpool to hockey over the weekend if Jake's mom could switch and do carpool home from the junior high today, instead. Then she put in a quick call to the PTA Vice President to beg off the meeting that evening. There was no way she could make it with Chloe sick. Yes, as soon as she got home she would email the agenda and the supporting documents over to the VP so she could run the meeting instead of Amanda.

As she pulled in to the parking lot of the elementary school, she heard a grating sound as the side of her wheel scraped the curb. "Oh, s%#@!" she exclaimed aloud. Craig was going to kill her. She had no time to take the car in to the shop this week. Amanda tried to put all that out of her mind as she raced in to pick up her sick kid, who she knew would need all of her attention for the rest of the day. She just didn't know how she was going to give it.

MODERN LIFE IS BUSY. WE ALL WANT TO ACHIEVE MORE IN A DAY, a week, a month. Children have soccer and piano and ballet and tae kwon do and SAT prep classes. Adults have committees and volunteer work and professional associations and cocktails after work and professional development events. We pack our lives full of activities because we're told that's the way to experience life to the fullest. The phrase "fear of missing out," or FOMO, has even become a part of the modern lexicon! We're so afraid to let life pass us by that we crash into bed at the end of the day exhausted and depleted, wondering where the time went.

On top of our busy schedules, we've also added technology to the overwhelm equation. Technology allows us to communicate more quickly when we want to, but it also allows other people to communicate with us when **they** want to. And they seem to want to—all day long. The separation between work and home life continues to get blurrier and blurrier, and our lives get busier and busier.

How do you know when you're in chaos mode? Do you feel paralyzed when you turn on your computer? Do you hear yourself snapping at your family? Do you find yourself defending your chaos-mode reactions, saying things like "Of COURSE I'm frustrated! I'm really stressed OUT right now!"? You aren't the only one—it happens a lot.

At my house, I know we're getting overwhelmed when the littlest problem elicits a great big reaction. My husband and I refer to it as turning a 2 into a 10—an incident that would normally rate as a 2 on the scale of irritating things, all of a sudden makes us respond with the anger and frustration that only a 10 should generate. And that overreaction is how we know we're in chaos mode.

Overreactions like this happen to all of us, and they're our warning system that we're totally overloaded. It's like the story about the straw that broke the camel's back—one tiny little piece of straw weighs nothing, but if the camel is almost at the breaking point, the addition of just a little more weight and he buckles. So many of us live our lives right on the edge of that breaking point anyway, so that when one more thing goes wrong, we don't have the mental or psychological capacity to cope with it. We simply snap, and become overwhelmed.

When we allow ourselves to be consumed by chaos, we are at great risk of burning out. The chaos of doing too much actually makes us **less** likely to solve our problems strategically and accomplish our goals. When we become overwhelmed, we spin our wheels, get frustrated with the lack of forward motion, and often fail to make headway on any of the things that are piling up on our plates.

Chaos feels normal in this day and age, but it doesn't have to be. In this chapter, I'm going to provide some strategies for you to use when you're feeling overwhelmed, so you can avoid dysfunctional coping amidst the chaos, pull yourself out of the spiral of overwhelm, and navigate panic mode successfully.

The Trials of Modern Life: Attention Deficit, Emotional Exhaustion, and Burnout

IN THE PAST SEVERAL YEARS, ATTENTION DEFICIT DISORDER HAS become a common part of our world, with many people learning to cope with a brain that focuses differently. While awareness of ADD is growing, focus is also being drawn to a less-severe but potentially more prevalent issue: Attention Deficit Trait. People suffering from Attention Deficit Trait have trouble juggling their schedules and focusing their priorities because they always feel overloaded. It's not quite as debilitating as a full-blown disorder, but Attention Deficit Trait can cause real issues in how well you cope with chaos.

But don't feel bad if you think this describes you! "ADT is our brains' natural response to exploding demands on our time and attention," according to research published in the Harvard Business Review. "The core symptoms are distractibility, inner frenzy, and impatience. The ADT sufferer therefore feels a constant low level of panic and guilt." Going from chaos to overwhelm to guilt is a downward spiral that gets tougher and tougher to pull out of.

In addition to the negative effects on our brains of being pulled in too many directions, another of the things that makes chaotic situations so stressful is the uncertainty associated with them. When will it end? How can I fix it? What do I do first? Problems created out of uncertainty can be among the hardest to solve, because they tend to set off your body's instinct to freeze. You don't know what to do, or what to do first, so your body wants to do nothing. Uncertainty can immobilize you, because you don't know what to anticipate.

Once you move out of the uncertainty period, that's when you often enter the "do something, anything," period. Now, your body and your mind really start to become overwhelmed. You frantically search for answers and solutions, trying to keep all the balls in the air. This experience is referred to as "emotional exhaustion." We almost all feel it at some point during our lives; no one is immune.

When the stressful conditions of life just won't let up, exhaustion is an almost guaranteed byproduct. As emotional exhaustion occurs, we've used up most of our emotional and physical resources for dealing with the problem or the stressful environment, and we start to give up. Once we consider giving up, we've officially reached the state of "burnout." Emotional exhaustion is, in fact, the key contributing factor to burnout.

Burnout is a scary word, particularly in the business world. Burnout is equated with high turnover intentions among staff, decreased motivation, and increased absenteeism, all things that companies want to avoid. In some studies, as many as two-thirds of U.S. employees reported being so stressed out at work they were planning to switch jobs. For you, as an individual, once burnout happens, it can be really hard to get yourself back into a productive state of mind. In fact, as your mind tries to protect yourself from the chaos through burnout and detachment, the chaos can seem even **more** overwhelming and impossible to overcome. Burnout is hard to recover from.

Despite the seeming downward spiral of it all, there are ways to cope with this kind of chaos in your life, and get it (and yourself) under control before you make it all the way to burnout. Well-meaning friends and family are apt to say things like "Just do one thing at a time," "Focus on the important stuff and just forget about everything else," or the ever-popular, "Well, you're just too busy. Next time, don't take on so many responsibilities." If you've ever heard those kinds of remarks, you know they only make you feel more stressed out, not less.

While the above are all decent, problem-focused ways to tackle a busy life, they don't actually make a dent on our psychological state of mind once we're already in the chaos cycle. Chaos and overwhelm actually block the problem-solving processes of our brain, so until we stop the spiral, the only way to go is down. Pulling yourself out of the spiral resembles doing what the fire-fighters used to tell you when they showed up at your elementary school: **Stop, Drop, and Roll.**

As a child, you learned that stop, drop, and roll is what you do if you catch fire by accident. First, you stop running, because fire thrives on oxygen. Second, you drop to the ground. When you are on the ground, you're taught to cover your face with your hands to prevent the flames from covering your face. Finally, you roll around on the ground, in an attempt to smother the flames and put them out. The stop, drop, and roll technique can both put out the fire, while also reducing the amount of injury the fire causes, but there is also a hidden second benefit. Stop, drop, and roll forces you to focus in a moment of panic. A routine you know by memory in your head can make you actually stop freaking out when you are on fire! That's pretty powerful stuff.

Use the same technique when you are figuratively on fire, to smother the chaos in your life.

Strategy: Stop

My dear friend Amber has a life anyone would marvel over. By her early 30s, she had two masters degrees, a husband and two beautiful children, a great job, and was an active community volunteer, serving on nonprofit boards and giving of her time and money. She accomplished more in a day than most people did in a week!

I asked her what her secret was to being so productive, and her answer surprised me.

"I've always been someone who does a lot," she responded. "But after my kids were born, I realized that I wasn't always doing things that **mean** a lot. One day it dawned on me that every 'yes' is a 'no' to something else. If I say yes to something, I'm saying no to something else, even if I don't know what it is at the time. Everything I take on takes me away from my kids, or my work, or something. I needed to make my time more meaningful, not more productive."

Amber realized that her life was quickly becoming too full to be enjoyable, and she learned how to master the first technique—stop. She quit adding more to her to-do list, because the things that were already on there (her family, her work, and the nonprofit board) were already the ones she wanted to prioritize.

Stopping is about more than just saying no to the next item on your to-do list, though. It's also about cutting out the dysfunctional behaviors that got you to this overwhelmed state in the first place. Perhaps you are someone who thinks that your lengthy list of obligations is a symbol of your worth. As Amber discovered, busy-ness is not equal to importance or positive effect. She had fallen into the habit of adding unimportant tasks to her to-do list, to the detriment of the really important things. She decided on the couple of arenas in her life where she really cared about being important, and the people she wanted to be important **to**, and refocused her time to align with those priorities.

Or maybe you hate to say no any time someone asks for your help. A lot of us fall into this trap, not wanting to seem disagreeable, unhelpful, or unlikable. If that sounds like you, it can help to realize that you are filling up your schedule with other people's desires, not your own. Are someone else's priorities worth more to you than your own? Are they worth more than your own sanity? When you take a moment and stop, you might realize that your precious hours are being spent crossing things off someone else's to-do list.

Perhaps you are just someone whose full calendar seems to have accumulated gradually, despite your attempts to slow it down. Most of us don't intentionally choose to invite chaos into our lives, it just builds as we add children, degrees, leadership, and community responsibilities to our already full plates. Lots of opportunities seem too good to refuse. If that sounds like you, stopping means stop trying to keep up with the overwhelming demands by accomplishing them! That seems counterintuitive, I know. But the frenetic pace of crossing a hundred things off your to-do list in a day doesn't stop the list from growing at the other end, does it? This is where you need to just take some time and hit the pause button. If you don't stop before you reach burnout, the spiral can get even harder to correct. So stop what you are doing, even for a single day, and you'll break the pattern. That's key to correcting the chaos.

A final way to "stop" is to cut out any dysfunctional coping strategies you may be relying on. Of all the stressful life situations, chaos seems to have the highest correlation to dysfunctional coping! Often people who are overwhelmed look for escape strategies, trying to cope by sleeping, watching television, or venting to friends. But those avoidance techniques often don't work to reduce stress in any situation, and they have been specifically shown not to reduce the stress caused by chaos.

What techniques can you use to stop yourself from slipping into the spiral of overwhelm?

1. **Freeze.** Make a conscious decision to step out of the spiral. Literally freeze in place if you have to! Even if it feels like the only way to solve this problem is to push through, by continuing on in the face of overwhelm, you're just getting in deeper. I know you want to accomplish just one more teeny tiny thing before you stop, but if you've reached that breaking point, you aren't doing yourself any good.

2. **Breathe.** It's okay to step away from your activity and give yourself a break for a few minutes. In fact, when you are feeling overwhelmed, you might be breathing rapidly and literally not getting enough oxygen, which in turn means you aren't thinking as clearly as you might need to be. Stepping away for a few minutes might feel like an indulgence you don't have time for, but you have to breathe in order to be able to control the chaos. A short mental break is not only helpful, but sometimes necessary, when you are feeling overwhelmed.

3. **Replace.** Trade out any dysfunctional coping habits for healthier ones. No matter how tempting it may be to check Facebook one more time, or turn on an episode of reality television, avoidance doesn't actually help you control the chaos. Instead, try something effective at mind-clearing, like exercise or spending time with friends (as long as you don't spend your time with them venting!).

LEADER'S
Toolbox

Controlling Chaos

MANY COMPANIES WOULD HATE TO ADMIT TO CHAOS IN their workplace. But BuildaSign.com's Dan Graham knows that the success of a fast-growing company relies on a little bit of upheaval. To become the world's largest online sign retailer in under 10 years, Graham and his employees have to be what he calls "okay with the gray," referring to not always having a clear cut answer.

To cope with the "gray," Graham says his employees rely on two things: their own business acumen, and what he calls "the best-presented information." Information gathering is a key element of reducing chaos, and BuildaSign.com educates its employees on how to get important information, while not getting so bogged down in the information that they forget to move forward. Calling it the "best-presented information" may be Graham's way of telling his employees that overwhelm can build if we gather **too** much information, and delay decision-making for too long.

BuildaSign.com employees have a digital way to beat the chaos, too: a software platform for developing and tracking professional development objectives and results. Graham says the software helps BuildaSign.com stay focused against competing priorities and what he calls "shiny object syndrome," where leaders want to chase the next breakthrough. By monitoring, tracking, and evaluating their progress on their big goals, BuildaSign.com employees know exactly what priorities are most important.

Though BuildaSign.com's environment of rapid growth and gray areas could cause overwhelm to employees, leadership minimizes the impact of the chaos on its employees with information, communication, and focus.

Leaders may express the sentiment that it isn't their job to make their employees feel less overwhelmed, but research shows employers who care about managing their teams' stress levels have lower burnout and less employee turnover. Turnover can cost companies up to 300% of the employee's salary, depending on the industry, so managing workplace overwhelm is actually a cost-saving measure.

As leaders, we can't always avoid chaos in our organizations, but we can respond in a way that protects our team members from the spiral of overwhelm, and gives our employees an easy way to control it when they start to get sucked into its orbit.

Strategy: Drop

During a workshop session I gave on controlling our response to frustration and overwhelm, the audience was taking some time to work together in pairs talking about their stressors and how they are currently handling frustrating situations in their lives. One pair of women motioned me over to them, and whispered that they wanted my advice.

One of the women, Diana, looked up at me with her eyes wide, and said, "My husband is sick, so I've had to add more hours to my work day to make up for his salary. But we have two kids, and my husband can't help as much since he got sick, and when I get home, I just panic. I don't even know where to start first. Do I start with dinner, or homework? When do I do the laundry? Do we even have food for me to make the kids lunch tomorrow?"

When there's too much to do and not enough time and information, your body can switch into crisis mode and send up an alarm trigger. Once that happens, your body and your mind are physically incapable of responding in a productive way. They need some time to slow down and reset, just like your home's burglar alarm sometimes needs to reset after it goes off. Diana's alarm system was definitely going off every evening when she arrived home and she felt paralyzed by all of the tasks awaiting her.

Taking a moment in the middle of the storm to calm yourself isn't avoiding the problem or wasting time. Research shows it's actually necessary if you want to get any useful work done. To accomplish this, you need to drop yourself into a lower gear. Doing so serves as a reset button for your brain. Short-term survival strategies are great for calming your mind down during this "drop" phase. What you want to look for are things you can do in-the-moment, that turn off the blaring "WE CAN'T DO THIS! WE'RE GOING DOWN" alarm that's sounding inside your head.

What techniques help you drop into a lower gear?

1. **Go with the flow state.** Try accomplishing simple tasks, like something you could do in your sleep. Perhaps it's time to rearrange your pantry or clean your closet! Experts recommend rote tasks like these, because they put you in "flow" state, and don't require too much mental energy. Repetitive tasks also work great here, like stamping envelopes.

2. **Have a little fun.** Choose an activity you enjoy that doesn't take too long, and have a little break for something fun, like playing a short game on your computer or reading a magazine article. These types of behaviors are called "avoidance tasks," and using them in situations like this can form bad habits if you rely on them too often. The trick, the experts say, is to only use them for a short period of time, probably no longer than 10 minutes, and not get sucked in and distracted for long. Remember, the whole purpose of this strategy is to ultimately be **more** productive, not less.

3. **Start small.** Completing the easiest piece of the overwhelming task can actually be a way to set yourself up for success. Have you heard the old joke: "How do you eat an elephant?" "One bite at a time!" Eating the elephant becomes easier when you break it into small pieces, and studies show that putting some structure (like a to-do list) around a big task can serve as a simple, less-intense way to start working on overwhelming activities. Pick a part of the overwhelming task that causes the least amount of pressure or mindfulness, that won't get your blood pressure rising already.

The key in this stage is that you've throttled back, you've dropped into a lower gear, and gotten your mind prepared for the chaos.

Strategy: Roll

Here's where you start rolling forward over these overwhelming situations! Unlike the short-term techniques above, that get you out of panic mode in the moment, those below are long-term techniques, taking days, weeks, or even months. But these techniques are how you'll start to make real change in how you manage chaotic situations.

Experts suggest you start controlling the chaos by gathering information about the problem at hand. Sometimes when we become overwhelmed, we skip the step of gathering information in our hurry to cross something off our list. But if we have all the information up front, we can often save ourselves time on the back end. Gathering information is a little bit like the way you start to roll forward on a bicycle—you can't be at full speed in the first few rotations. Spend a few moments gearing up as you start to roll forward, and gather your information as you begin to move.

Studies show that having an internal locus of control at this point is also a benefit. In Chapter 1, we talked about the benefits of having an internal locus of control, where you feel like you have power over the things that happen to you. Chaotic situations can make you feel like you've lost all control, so developing that internal locus of control helps you stay calm in overwhelming situations.

Another successful tactic to cope with overwhelm appears to be social support. Whether a college student or a CEO, those people who had more social resources – friends, family, colleagues, etc. – were better able to control their stress in the middle of chaotic situations. We've already covered the benefits of social support for other struggles, like managing change. When you're dealing with chaos, social support offers you perspective, so you no longer feel like you are the only one who is overwhelmed.

Be aware, however, that in seeking out the support of other people, it's key to avoid "venting." There is a fine line between having constructive conversations that lead to productive advice, and venting just to rehash or ruminate on an issue. Venting is dangerous for two reasons: not only does it keep you thinking about a problem over and over, but it also allows you to release just enough steam that you don't have the motivation you need to make changes to your situation. Venting has actually proven to be a debilitating strategy that keeps you stuck in place! So when you seek social support, be sure that you aren't venting, rather receiving productive support from others.

What techniques help you to roll forward in the face of an overwhelming and chaotic situation?

1. **Inform yourself.** Gathering information is the first step in problem-focused coping for any problem. Choose the thing that seems to be consuming most of your time, or feels most overwhelming, and spend some time researching ways to improve it, manage it better, or get it done in less time. For example, you might learn ways to control your email inbox, or make meetings more productive. Time **is** a precious resource, particularly when you are overwhelmed, but if you spend some time gathering as much information as possible about the problem and the environment, you may see some new solutions emerge to help you get the chaos under control.

2. **Gain control.** Shift your focus to the things that you can control and have controlled, and spend your time and attention on those things first, to reinforce your belief that you are in control of the tasks at hand. When the voice starts to creep in that says, "No matter what you do, you'll never be able to make an impact on all of this," quiet it with reminders of all the things you have accomplished.

3. **Seek support.** Find a mentor, friends, or colleagues who can keep your thoughts productive and in perspective. Use your emotional supporter as a sounding board and a buffer, but not as an outlet for venting. Having great social support is one of the best long-term strategies for not getting overwhelmed by the pressures of life, so keep them close at hand when things start to get overwhelming.

A Final Thought on Controlling Chaos

We all overcome stressful situations every single day. More and more, however, our stressors seem to be out of control. Modern life feels somehow bigger, like we live in several dimensions at the same time: not just work and home, but online, with friends, or volunteering in the community. We're constantly taking off one hat and putting on another, just to get through everything on our to do list. Managing chaos is difficult for most of us, yet we can do it in three simple steps.

To control chaos in your life:

- **Stop.** Push pause on the insanity, and stop the cycle. Also put an end to any dysfunctional coping you might have been using

- **Drop.** Pull back into a lower gear, allowing your body and your mind a chance to reset from the panic mode

- **Roll.** Slowly begin to make headway against your tasks, in a mindful way. Make sure you have an internal locus of control and strong social support, to avoid falling back into the chaos trap

MANAGING CONFLICT

IF DAVID INTERRUPTED HER AGAIN, SHE WAS GOING TO SCREAM. At every staff meeting, Dana felt like David talked over her, belittled her ideas, and denigrated her in front of her bosses. This time he was telling management that her approach to handling one of their long-time clients was going to cost them money. And they were actually believing him!

David cornered her after the meeting. "There's no way this is going to fly, Dana. You've really screwed the pooch on this one. You ought to just hand the reigns over to me so I can show you how **real** work gets done around here," he chuckled, as he walked back to his desk. Dana's face turned red as she watched his retreating back. The client loved her, and it used to be her favorite project to work on, but David was making her life miserable.

Ever since Dana had come up with a creative solution to one of the company's problems with getting information out to clients in a timely manner, David had seemed to resent her. He had only been with the company six months longer than she had, but he treated her as if she were an interloper. At first, she thought he was that way with everyone, but it became obvious that he was targeting her, in particular.

At the advice of her husband, Dana brought the hostility up to her boss during a review period. "Well, that's just his way," the manager placated her. "He's just really aggressive about doing good work, and it comes across as being rude. He doesn't mean it. Besides, it's pushing you to do great work. You've had your best quarter yet! Maybe you should be thanking David!"

She didn't want to keep bothering her supervisor about it, when he obviously didn't want to hear it. Besides she was worried it would make her look like a complainer, or like she couldn't get along with her teammates. At first, Dana tried to just ignore him, but it didn't stop. The more Dana ignored him, the worse she felt he got. First he was calling her to the table at staff meetings, then David started responding to emails the client was copied on, bringing up things Dana "needed to be sure to do," as though she had forgotten. And as though he was her boss!

It was the last straw. She charged over to David's desk with a printout of the email. "What are you trying to pull here, David? Why are you trying to make me look bad in front of my client?" She slammed the email down on his desk and waited for an answer.

WE'VE ALL EXPERIENCED FRICTION BETWEEN OURSELVES AND someone else. Maybe it's your colleague who just rubs you the wrong way, or is always trying to one-up you. Maybe you are deadlocked with your spouse or partner on an issue neither one of you is willing to budge on. Or maybe you have a teenager in your house, and there seems to be conflict 24 hours a day, but you aren't even sure what the problem is!

Conflict can be a natural and healthy thing. When I was in high school, I had a teacher who once told us, "As teenagers, you are supposed to be fighting with your parents right now. If you and your parents didn't make life difficult for one another, you'd never leave home and make a family of your own and continue the species." Unfortunately, though, conflict rarely *feels* healthy.

Conflict can block us from productive activities, because our energy is spent on the struggle. Our brains register a threat to our well-being, and respond by directing attention and focus to the conflict situation. But hyper-focus on the conflict often results in the situation becoming magnified in our minds. In addition to mentally increasing the conflict, we also run the risk of minimizing or neglecting the other elements of our lives that aren't in conflict. When we ignore the healthy parts of our lives in favor of focusing on the conflicted parts, we feed the conflict.

Throughout this chapter, I'll explain the difference between helpful and dysfunctional conflict, show you the top techniques for finding mutually beneficial solutions, and help you positively re-engage in a conflict-ripe environment.

Good Conflict, Bad Conflict

Other people don't think the same way you do. They don't work the same way you do. They don't value the same things you do. For all those reasons and more, conflict is a stressor just waiting to happen.

When you are able to smoothly act on your desires, beliefs, or plans, all feels right with the world. Things are going your way! But sometimes you run across someone else who has opposing desires, beliefs, or plans. And sometimes that person can't just be ignored, because their desires, beliefs and plans are standing in the way of you getting what you want. Perhaps they are your boss, spouse, colleague, or child. That's the moment when the match of conflict is lit.

In the right situations and when handled properly, some conflict can produce great outcomes—better solutions, a chance to connect with our passions, or an opportunity to clarify our thinking.

Whether conflict works or not actually depends on the **quality** of the conflict, not the quantity. Healthy conflict, the experts tell us, is usually task related—disagreements over tasks, processes and procedures. Conflict of this type can even be necessary, because the incorporation of different opinions makes for a healthy and more robust solution. It helps groups of people (and even couples) come up with productive ways of behaving and working that minimize future disagreement.

Although task-related conflict can be good, there are limits. One report of conflict-management in the workplace suggests that about 20% of a manager's time is spent moderating disagreements. And when conflict becomes the norm rather than the exception, it leads to turnover, absenteeism, and burned out employees.

But because of less-than-ideal circumstances and poor management, most of the conflict we experience leaves us feeling hurt, belittled, emotionally exhausted, and unable to move on. When our thoughts and feelings are challenged or dismissed, how can we not take it personally? Typically when this happens, we have shifted over into or are dealing with people-related conflict.

Unlike task-related conflict, people-related conflict is personal. It deals with a difference of values, norms, and ways of behaving. People-related conflict doesn't tend to move the combatants closer to a solution. In fact, the longer a people-related conflict goes on, the less likely it can be that a solution will be found.

But here's the kicker: research suggests that most people can't tell the difference between task-related conflict and people-related conflict! Particularly when you're one of the participants, it becomes impossible to tell which type of conflict you are in. Both types of conflict **feel** personal to the people involved. David Rock's SCARF model, which you were introduced to in the chapter on reclaiming power and control, suggests that conflict often arises as a result of a perceived threat to our status. This threat can emerge in task- or people-related conflicts. When someone disagrees with us or corrects us, our brain actually responds the same way it would if we were under physical threat. Status threats can even make our brain think that we are experiencing physical pain! Obviously, then, conflict can be incredibly stressful, difficult to manage, and difficult to differentiate, because our brain is overloaded by a threat response.

They also both feel like they can be solved, if the other person would just give in (and how many times have you seen **that** happen?). When we're in conflict with someone else, every cell in our body is screaming that the other person should change. They should be different! They should think different! But that line of thought won't actually solve the conflict. Research done in 2000, in fact, recommends "employees facing high conflict, high stress environments may be able to shape that environment by modifying their approach to conflict." Modifying their own approach was what worked, not changing the other person. In fact, when faced with conflict, we can't change the other person or their position without changing our own tactics along the way.

The first thing we have to change is how we think about the conflict. Whether conflict appears at work, at home, or among friends, it can feel almost impossible to mediate. You can walk away from the situation, only to find yourself sitting on the sofa hours later, thinking, "I wish I had said **that**! I sure should have come back with something wittier. I should have done **this**. I wish I could have put them in their place." Conflict can get us locked in rumination about what we should have done, what we wish we could do, and how "bad" the other person is.

Rumination is what happens when reflection – which is a positive resilience tool – crosses the line into dwelling. Rumination can be recognized because not only will your brain be on autoloop, but you'll also find yourself stuck thinking only about the past, not the future. So both the quantity of your thoughts and the quality of your thoughts are impacted when you ruminate. Some psychological studies suggest that excessive rumination can actually lead to depression. Interestingly, an individual could have a major catastrophe, but not be dwelling on it, and they'll be psychologically healthier than someone who had a much less critical event but just can't put it out of their head. Getting stuck ruminating can be common when dealing with conflict, but because it blocks you from moving forward, it's important to get past it. We'll discuss even more about avoiding rumination in the chapter on rejection.

When we're faced with conflict, we want to do two things: make the conflict go away (get past it), while simultaneously feeling like we've benefited from the solution. In order to accomplish both desires, we need to first determine if the conflict we're locked in is task-related or people-related and then apply the right strategies for the situation.

Strategy: Ask Yourself, Is This a Clash of Personalities or a Difference of Opinions?

When caught in a conflict, it can feel nearly impossible to know if the conflict is personal or it isn't. Both task-related conflict and people-related conflict feel personal, even though only people-related conflict is. To resolve a conflict or handle it successfully, we have to attempt to determine which conflict is present: task-related or people-related. Step away from the situation momentarily, and reflect. Recognize if the situation causing the conflict is based on procedures, or on people.

Some conflict arises from differences of opinions. These task-related conflicts aren't personal at all. You can identify a task-related conflict because it is often process- or policy-oriented. If the root of the conflict a disagreement about **how** to do something, the conflict is likely a task-related conflict. You and the person or people you disagree with both want the same thing, but just don't agree on how to get it.

On the other hand, if you and the other person (or people) just can't speak the same language, you likely are experiencing people-related conflict. In a people-related conflict, you may feel that there is no common ground at all. You may not just disagree on strategies or tactics—you can't come to an agreement on goals, values, or vision at all. Some research suggests that this type of people-related conflict emerges when task-related conflicts go unresolved for long periods of time.

What techniques can you use to determine if a conflict is task-related or people-related?

1. **Get some distance.** Try to step away from the situation as much as possible. It can be helpful to seek advice from a trusted advisor or friend, to offer an outsider's opinion on the root of the conflict.

2. **Reflect.** Ask yourself:
   - "What is being challenged? Is the other person challenging my ideas, or are they challenging the core of who I am?"
   - "Do we agree on the goal, just not the ways to achieve it?"
   - "What does the other person want to achieve? Do they want to achieve success, or do they want to injure my ego?"
   - "Who can win? Is there a way we can both have success in this situation, or will they not be satisfied unless I 'lose'?"
   - "When did this conflict arise? Has it always been like this, or is the conflict rooted in a specific situation that will end at some point?"

Strategy: Tackle Task Conflict By Building Regard

Ron's role as the president of the board of directors for a nonprofit had been fun, when he started. Even though it meant some long hours, and serving on a board was a volunteer job that didn't pay, Ron loved helping the organization and giving back to the community. But lately it was starting to be a lot less fun.

Ron had started butting heads with Karen, the board treasurer, six weeks earlier. Karen wanted the organization to start setting money aside for an endowment fund, which would allow the organization to have a nest egg for the future. Ron felt that starting an endowment fund this year would be risky, because the organization needed fluid capital for the program that had just launched six months earlier. As he walked into the next board meeting, he was worrying over what he felt was about to happen.

"Ron!" Karen exclaimed during the financial report, "I keep the books. I see the money going in and out every single day! I know what we can afford."

"Whether we can afford it right now or not isn't what I'm concerned about, though, Karen," Ron replied. "I'm concerned that if something happens to this new program, we'd have all our money tied up in an endowment. With no way to fund the program, we'd have to kill it. For an organization as new as we are, the failure of a program we've hyped up so much would be terrible press, and our clients would quit trusting us."

"I don't understand why you don't trust me, Ron. Do you think I'm not doing a good job as treasurer? If you don't think I am, why don't you just replace me?!?!"

Ron could tell the argument was going downhill, but didn't know what to say.

"I think you are doing a great job as treasurer, Karen."

"Then why don't you think I have the organization's best interest at heart?"

Ron realized that Karen **did** have the organization's best interests at heart. She wasn't intending to fight Ron. She was advocating for what she thought was best, and so was Ron.

When a conflict is task-related, like Ron's and Karen's, the solution can be found by looking at two variables: your concern for yourself, and your concern for the other person. If you are highly concerned for yourself, but have no concern for others, conflict leads to you forcing your will on the other person. If you have low concern for yourself and a great deal of concern for others, you're likely to give in and accept whatever the other person wants. If you have low concern for both yourself and the other side, you'll probably just avoid both the conflict and your feelings about it. And finally, if you have a high concern for yourself **and** a high concern for the other parties, you'll find yourself solving the problem.

In this situation, it's best to focus on the tactics, not the personalities. Do this by gathering information. Remember, information-seeking is one of the most common tactics in problem-focused coping. The purpose of the information should be to broaden your perspective: to help you see why the conflict arose in the first place, and why the other parties hold the views they do. This constructive information then informs how you can deploy the two-variable concept, of having high regard for both yourself and for the other person.

Information gathering may be easier said than done when you are in the middle of a conflict with someone. It doesn't feel like you can just sit down over a cup of coffee with someone if you just got finished with a major argument. It often helps to start the process alone. Get in a neutral frame of mind and start challenging yourself to see the other person's perspective. Once you are able to visualize their point of view, even in the smallest way, it will likely become easier to dial the confrontation back a notch the next time you find yourself face-to-face with the person with whom you are locked in conflict. Studies even show that a single positive interaction between two people can be all it takes for the parties to start finding a solution together.

The above technique truly works, however, only if the conflict is task-related. If a conflict is born out of personalities, then something as tactical as the two-variable concept won't matter, because the people involved don't have a high regard for one another. In that case, the solution becomes more complicated.

When you can have a high regard for another person's opinion while not letting go of your own high regard for your own opinion, that's when problem-solving happens. Develop a passionate belief that both opinions can be honored in the solution, and not only will the conflict go away, but the best possible solution to the problem is likely to emerge.

What techniques help to build the regard necessary for diffusing task-related conflict?

1. **Walk in their shoes.** To have high regard for the other person, begin to develop a high consideration for the other point of view. Why does what they believe matter? How does their perspective inform their opinion? How could their point of view contribute to a healthy outcome? Remind yourself all along the way that their disagreement with your perspective isn't personal.

2. **Ask questions.** Gather information to help you understand why the other person might think the way they do. Find out what the other person is prioritizing that makes them see the situation from a different angle. If you have done a successful job of walking in their shoes and seeing things from their point of view, you then can find a higher regard for their beliefs and positions.

3. **Keep believing.** As you gain a respect for the opposing beliefs, continue to hold a high regard for your own position, as well. Remind yourself why you believe what you do, because the why matters more than the how when trying to get to a win-win.

Strategy: Tackle People Conflict by Engaging

Johanna stared at her cell phone, knowing it was about to ring. Every time she got off the phone with her sister, she knew she would call back five minutes later for another round of arguing. Even though they were adults with their own families, Michaela still knew how to push Johanna's buttons every single time.

The phone call hadn't gone well. Her sister had been complaining about her job, as usual. Johanna had tried to help, as usual. But as usual, Michaela twisted Johanna's words, making them out to be some sort of insult.

"Are you saying my job isn't good enough?" Michaela challenged.

"No, not at all. I was just trying to help. I know Joe's office is looking for someone and I thought you might be a good fit."

"You're so embarrassed that I'm just a secretary! Well if I'm not good enough for you, then my kids probably aren't good enough for you! You can forget about me bringing them over next weekend for Thanksgiving."

Johanna's heart ached every time Michaela threatened not to let her see her niece and nephew after a fight. She loved those kids. But maybe it wasn't worth it to keep arguing with Michaela. It stressed her out so much. Maybe she should just cancel Thanksgiving. Ever since Mom died it wasn't the same, anyway.

As the phone rang, Johanna wondered if this was it. Would this be the conversation where she finally told Michaela, "Forget it. I'm not your punching bag any more. Good bye!"

If you're in a tough, emotion-ridden conflict and you've taken a good hard look at the problem, and the problem is definitely being caused by personalities, you have a complicated puzzle ahead of you. People-related conflicts are often more difficult to solve than task-related conflicts, because you and the other person lack a common goal or common values from which to begin to build regard for one another.

People-related conflicts can also feel more intentional. Sometimes these conflicts **are** intentional, and the other person is purposely trying to be a threat to you or cause you harm in order to get what they want or cause you to give up. Other times, the person isn't trying to be hurtful, offensive, or aggressive, but their personality simply clashes with yours in a way that raises your hackles.

Individuals locked in people-related conflict are more likely to have high levels of annoyance. In fact, large conflict can often be looked at as the sum total of several little annoyances that build up into a single, overwhelming feeling of dislike, much like how we as children at the arcade handed over our little toys and traded up to one giant prize. Sometimes this is more an issue of perspective than reality, though.

The extent to which you can keep the current problem in perspective, and not cloud the issue with past disagreements, determines how well you will be able to move forward. When you globalize a conflict, expecting that the same conflict will always exist or roping all past disagreements into it, you are doing more than just making an assessment, you are actually feeding the growth of the problem. Reduce the globalization you may be feeling around the problem. Focus only on this particular conflict, at this point in time.

A common outcome of major conflict, which usually means people-related conflict, is detachment and depersonalization. We feel more comfortable when we pull away, and we come to view the people we're facing off against as less than human. These techniques make you feel better in the short term, but they're poor long-term strategies to managing conflict. In fact, when you detach from conflict, you become passive. Just as in task-related conflict, passivity predicts a poorer outcome. When studies were done of employees who yielded in the face of a disagreement, the results clearly showed that people who disengaged from conflict received a short-term increase in well-being, but a long-term **decrease**.

Because people-related conflict often causes detachment, your #1 priority is therefore to remain engaged. Engaged with work, or your relationship, or whatever the root of the conflict is. Just like Johanna felt in her conflict with her sister, conflict makes us want to pull away and quit trying, but we have to fight that urge.

Re-engaging in an environment that has been a source of conflict is a tall order. We don't want to commit more of ourselves to something that is painful. But think about it: it wouldn't be so painful if you didn't care about some aspect of the environment. Sometimes, overcoming conflict takes completely rethinking the way we see that environment. It can help to set new goals, so that you can start over with a fresh set of eyes. Another important element in staying engaged is remembering not to depersonalize the other member(s) of the conflict. The more you do depersonalize, the more difficult it will become to stay engaged in a healthy solution. Finally, find the support you need in order to stay engaged.

What techniques help you stay engaged during a people-related conflict?

1. **Get goal-focused.** When you set new goals around a conflict-laden situation, you let go of old goals that might have negative feelings attached to them. Setting new goals also gives you a way to refocus and re-engage in a new and positive way. It can help to set goals that, at least in the short term, give you some distance from the environment or personalities behind the conflict, if possible.

2. **They're people, too.** Resist the urge to depersonalize the person or people with whom you are facing the conflict. Challenge yourself to recall some personal facts about the other party, like the name of their spouse or children, or their favorite hobby. By focusing on the things that make that person a person instead of just an adversary, you are more likely to keep the conflict healthy and avoid depersonalization.

3. **Stay attached.** Several methods exist to help you stay engaged. If the conflict is at work, find a mentor or coach who can offer support. Continue to participate in meetings, and contribute your ideas to the conversation. Even find another project to stay engaged in, if you have to, in order to be as fully engaged as possible in your workplace. At home, methods for avoiding detachment include taking up a new hobby, enjoying weekend activities together, having constructive conversations, and completing projects together. Maybe you take up a volunteer activity or do something new that the other person has been dying to try. Avoid turning on the television or computer, and retreating to your separate spaces. Remember, passive behaviors like that might avoid a confrontation in the moment, but lead to worse problems in the long term.

A Final Thought About Managing Conflict

Staying attached to your goals, your values, and your desired outcome during a conflict doesn't cause fighting, it can actually lead to a healthy solution, when done correctly. When your attachment to the outcome is positive and not stubborn, you will have a more likely shot at reducing the conflict, solving the problem that is the underlying cause, **and** walking away from the conflict with minimal battle scars.

LEADER'S
Toolbox

Supporting Healthy Workplace Conflict

CONFLICT IN THE WORKPLACE CAN SPELL DOOM FOR AN organization's growth. Office conflict, both task-related and people-related, leads to absenteeism, staff turnover, and poor collaboration and project outcomes. Unsurprisingly, employees who work around high levels of conflict are dissatisfied with their jobs.

Research shows managers can combat the negative effects of workplace conflict by modeling "constructive controversy." When a conflict is task-oriented, leadership should highlight the positive, problem-solving and idea-generating benefits of such disagreements. At the same time, it is also helpful to pay special attention to the shared goals of the team, and keep the focus on the outcome of achieving those goals.

People-related conflict in the workplace can be trickier to manage. Some managers may feel that it is not their place to address "personal disagreements." But letting these struggles linger often leads to escalated conflict and almost always results in staff turnover. Keeping employees engaged in their roles can become difficult, but managers can intervene by providing support for their employees (either their own support or that of someone outside the team). Organizational support has been shown to have a strong buffering effect in the face of workplace conflict, and in certain studies, was the highest predictor of continued employee engagement.

Many successful companies have core values as part of their business model, but Accenture's commitment to their core values is woven into the fiber of everything they do. Accenture is a consulting and outsourcing company. Their professional services are aimed at increasing productivity and efficiency for their clients across the globe, and they believe their core values are a part of their business offerings.

One of their most cherished core values is "respect for the individual." At Accenture, individual respect means, among other techniques, coming up with innovative ways to support and communicate with every employee. Employees are given a career coach – usually in addition to their supervisor or manager – in order to have someone in their corner to help guide their career and navigate problems or conflict.

Career coaches at Accenture are trained to help employees navigate their challenges, including providing an objective opinion to help employees find constructive, rather than destructive, ways of looking at conflict. Without a career coach, employees might feel compelled to vent their frustrations to their supervisors, which can be detrimental to both team morale and an employee's career growth. One successful purpose the Accenture career coaches provide is a safe sounding board to put conflict into perspective. That kind of organizational support may be rare, but studies show it is one of the best strategies to keep workplace friction productive.

By getting individuals engaged with their coaches, Accenture is solving several problems: first, objective advice from coaches can help employees figure out the root of the problems, and whether the conflict traces back to tasks or people. Whatever the root of the problem, coaches provide a human connection, which leads to greater connection to the organization, thereby avoiding detachment. When Accenture employees have a problem, they know the first place to go is to their coach, thereby getting them engaged more deeply in the organization and more committed to the outcome. An organization without such a program risks employees having nowhere to turn, pulling away, and therefore detaching.

To determine if a conflict is task-related or people-related, try asking yourself:

- "Do we have the same end goal, just different ways of getting there?"
- "Would this person have the same conflict with someone else who shared my point of view, or is it just me?"

To build regard for someone when you are locked in a task-related conflict, try:

- Building regard for their point of view by considering their perspective
- Gathering information about their position
- Remembering to maintain your high consideration for your own point of view, at the same time

To stay engaged when you are locked in a people-related conflict, try:

- Refocusing on goals and priorities surrounding the conflicted environment

- Resisting the urge to depersonalize the person or people with whom you are facing the conflict

- Retaining your attachments. Avoid the instinct to detach from the conflict and the people involved

SURVIVING REJECTION

COLIN KNEW HE HAD DONE EVERYTHING HE COULD TO DESERVE this promotion. He had spent the past two years putting in extra face time with clients. He mentored younger staff members. He worked on Saturdays to get big projects finished. He golfed with the bosses. Heck, for three months he had even been doing the job of the vacant VP-level position on his team. Walking in to his supervisor's office, he knew today was the day he was going to hear the news.

"Colin, have a seat," the HR rep said.

Colin sat, looking at the three faces around him and wishing they could get to the good part.

"Colin, we know you expressed interest in the vice president role. We want you to know that we considered all your years of expertise and your dedication to the company. But we decided to go with someone else."

Colin's ears started buzzing, and he barely heard another word his bosses said.

How could they not have picked him? Who could they have picked that would be better? Surely nobody worked harder than he did? Nobody cared more about the company. Nobody knew all the ins and outs like he did.

Colin stumbled out of his supervisor's office and down the hall to his desk. His face was stinging with embarrassment. He couldn't even remember if he had said anything to his bosses as he left. He picked up his phone and dialed his wife.

"Did it happen?!?!" Jessica asked, as soon as she picked up the line. "Did you get it?!?!"

Colin's throat closed up and he could barely murmur "No." He had wanted to hear his wife's voice, to have her comfort him, but now he wished he hadn't called her. He was ashamed to tell her he didn't get the promotion. He sat there on the line without saying anything, just looking at the picture of Jessica and his three kids. Had he completely let them down?

WE'RE ALL DRIVEN TO BELONG. EVEN THE INTROVERTS AMONG us, who need time alone, still rest secure in the knowledge that they belong somewhere, that they have "their people." In some way, shape, or form, we all like to feel a part of something greater than ourselves. And when that belonging is threatened by rejection, we feel pain. When we feel rejected, we naturally pull away to protect ourselves. But in doing so, we become more fragile in our dealings with others, and even more vulnerable to future perceived rejections.

In this section, you will learn the three statements you need to tell yourself to manage the sting of rejection and avoid the trap of reacting to rejection in ineffectual ways.

Rejection Can Hurt and Help at the Same Time

Struggling with rejection is a primal feeling. In fact, when we are rejected, our brains often go into caveman mode.

Studies of rejection show that people who are forced out of a group have trouble with higher-order cognitive processing. Simple activities, like daily tasks, are fine, but the more delicate cognitive processes of the brain become impaired. When we are rejected, our brain stops making connections between ideas, and becomes poor at interpreting other people's meanings: all those sensitive, modern tasks our brain is supposed to take care of for us. When someone threatens our sense of belonging, we're like primal cavemen again.

One reason is that when we're rejected our cortisol levels also rise, causing us to feel stress. Cortisol is a stress hormone, the one that's responsible for sending you into fight-or-flight mode. Certainly there are times when cortisol is necessary, but increased cortisol as a result of a rejection can often trigger an overreaction. So our brains *and* our bodies respond negatively to being rejected.

Dealing with rejection can make us hyper-sensitive to rejection in the future. It makes sense that our bodies and brains would want to protect us from the cortisol-flooding and the brain-func-tion-break-down—they don't want to go through that again! But when we remain insecure about future rejections, we're always on the lookout for signs that rejection is coming. This can create a self-fulfilling prophecy: we're worried someone will reject us, so we perceive the slightest triggers in another person's behavior as possible rejection, and we jump to the conclusion that we're being rejected, which causes us to react poorly or inappropriately in the circumstances. If we're overly-sensitive about rejection, we can behave in off-putting ways that cause other people to reject us. Isn't *that* ironic?

Despite how hard we try to avoid it, rejection doesn't actually have to be all that bad for us. Several studies of authors and researchers who had submitted their writings show that rejection actually improved the end product. After several rounds of rejec-tion, the papers and books that ultimately get published had a higher overall value and were rated objectively better works than the earlier drafts. Another benefit authors saw when their papers were rejected was that they got better at selecting the appropriate venue to which they would submit their writing. Many authors at the beginning of their career send a project to a hundred different places, but as the rejections and critiques come in, the authors get better and better about targeting the right publications. Rejection can actually help us find the places where we are appreciated. If we are open to learning the lesson, rejection actually helps **us**, the rejected, become more discriminating, as we seek to affiliate with the people and groups who are the best match for us.

When faced with rejection, whether on the job, while looking for a job, looking for a mate, or just looking for friends, it is important to recognize that your body and your brain may be working against you. Because your sense of belonging is threatened, your brain is reduced to lower-order, primitive processing. Your perception is threatened, and your fight-or-flight instincts kick in. These reactions work to your detriment, but they're hard to control. So first, cut yourself some slack. Let yourself go into caveman mode for a little bit, if that's what it takes.

As long as you recognize that you've gone into caveman (or cavewoman!) mode, you'll be better able to adapt accordingly. Denial is the worst thing you can do at this point. It's helpful to recognize that your functioning has been impaired by the rejection, but the response is only temporary. Acknowledge that you may be overly sensitive to rejection for a while, but some of that is just your perception, not reality. Take a little time to let your body and brain absorb the situation, then you can start the resilience and recovery process.

The process for surviving rejection should look like this:

1. "It isn't personal."
2. "It wasn't that great anyway."
3. "It doesn't matter."

Of the three techniques that help with surviving rejection, shifting your perspective away from the personal is the only one that also works during other stressful situations. The other two techniques that work for rejection should actually be **avoided** at all costs when dealing with other types of struggle.

Those simple three sentences can make a world of difference in how you bounce back when used appropriately. But let's break them down a little further, so you can see how to get there.

Strategy: Shift Your Perspective from the Personal

This is your brain on rejection: *"This rejection is all my fault. I'm unwanted, unlikeable, un-hire-able, etc."*

This is what you want your brain to say, instead: *"It isn't personal."*

Lydia ducked into the coffee shop after dropping off the twins at day care. As she stood in line, she heard a familiar voice behind her and turned around. At a table by the door sat three of her neighbors. All around her age, all with children near the twins' age.

Lydia had just hosted the neighborhood block party a few weeks earlier. She thought they were her friends, or at least that they all were friendly. But here the women were, and no one had invited Lydia. She wondered whether she should say hello to them as she walked out, or if that would be too embarrassing.

Why hadn't they invited her? Had she said something to offend someone at the block party? Had one of the twins bitten one of their kids? Did they judge her because she didn't stay at home full time? Lydia knew rationally that she didn't want to be friends with women who didn't want to be friends with her, but she still wanted to be included.

Often, we tell ourselves that rejection is personal. But studies show that rejection usually isn't as personal as we feel it to be, so we can improve our mental state by shifting our perspective. When we take things too personally, it's an error of our explanatory style, the way we explain why things happen to us. Someone with a negative explanatory style believes that negative things happen because they deserve it. They take it personally. When you automatically jump to the conclusion that rejection is a personal indictment of you, you'll find it harder to cope and move on.

When sales people are trained to help manage sales call anxiety, one of the first things they're taught is that rejection isn't personal. You never know what the person on the other end of the line is dealing with right now. Perhaps their spouse is in the hospital. Perhaps their credit card was just stolen. Almost 40% of salespeople will experience intense anxiety over rejection at some point in their careers, but they are taught to cope by shifting their perspective away from the personal sting of resentment. What they are taught to focus on instead is reality, in the form of their past sales successes and their current close ratios. The reality of those facts and figures is something within their control, and those numbers aren't personal, they're just numbers.

Recognizing that rejection is often not personal is one of the key predictors of success, particularly in careers like sales or entrepreneurship, where rejection can be a regular part of the cycle. But it's equally important in our personal lives. Start working on your explanatory style. Remind yourself that it isn't personal, and you'll be in a better position to move on.

What techniques can be used to shift your perspective and not take rejection as personally as it feels?

1. **Correct yourself.** When you hear your inner voice tell you that the rejection is all your fault, and yours alone, stop the voice. Figure out a new story you can repeat in your head, instead. Try thinking things like "I didn't get what I wanted, and that stings. I'm not entirely certain why it didn't happen for me this time. The other person/people made decisions based on their knowledge and values, and I guess it didn't match up." You

often don't know all the real reasons a rejection happened, so don't try to fill in the blanks and assume the rejection is personal. Not only is that not the truth, but continuing to believe it is damaging to your future success.

2. **Think about the past.** Bring to mind the things you excel at, and you'll be beefing up your self-esteem. There was a time in the past when you were successful and you achieved what you wanted. Reflect on that time, and remind yourself that success is possible for you. Think about the circumstances surrounding that success. Not only will you feel better emotionally, but you may uncover some clues to help you be more successful in your current situation.

3. **Get by with a little help from your friends.** To stop taking rejection personally, it helps to surround yourself with people and situations who are appreciative of you. If some people embrace you, then the rejection of others can't be because you are personally undesirable!

Strategy: Minimize the Importance

This is your brain on rejection: *"I just got rejected from the best thing ever. Something this amazing will never come along again."*

This is what you want your brain to say, instead: *"It wasn't that great anyway."*

Remember, of the three strategies described in this chapter, only one also works during other stressful situations. The other two, minimizing the importance and distracting yourself, are dangerous in other contexts and should be avoided. Let's dive into minimization first.

Author Kathryn Stockett received wide acclaim for her first novel, *The Help*. But before *The Help* became a bestseller, Stockett received 60 rejection letters. As the letters piled up, her friends and family, while supportive of her efforts to be a writer, suggested that perhaps she move on to other things, like start a new book. But Stockett persisted. In the back of her head was a voice saying *someone, somewhere, is going to love this book as much as I do.*

Despite the feedback of 60 literary agents, Stockett had no intention of giving up. Though 60 people didn't like the book, she felt they were wrong. She credits her own stubbornness with keeping her going until she found agent #61. Agent #61 loved *The Help*, and Stockett finally sold the book. Had Stockett believed the feedback of the first 60 people she encountered, the world would have never gotten a much-beloved book.

Minimization is a technique that **only** works to help you cope with rejection. When it comes to rejection, minimization means you discount the importance of the rejection. Perhaps you tell yourself, "It wasn't that great anyway," or "Those people don't know what they're talking about." In studies of people who weren't chosen to be a part of a group, the study participants explained afterward that not only did they not want to be chosen by the group, but that the people who selected them clearly didn't have good leadership skills and weren't the kind of group they would want to be a part of, anyway. That attitude is called "derogation," basically minimizing the extent to which you wanted to be included in the first place.

By derogating the people who rejected us, and minimizing how much the rejection means, we allow ourselves to brush off the pain that rejection can sometimes cause. One of the most destructive ways we can handle rejection is by globalizing the hurt we feel, and blowing it up to be an all-important part of our lives. Have you ever seen someone do that? "This was the PERFECT job for me—I'll never get another chance at this dream job." Or "She was the best girlfriend ever. There's no one else like her. I don't think I'll ever get over losing her."

While most resilience strategies for other struggles involve being honest with yourself, this situation is one that can call for a little clever reframing of the situation. When we tell ourselves that the opinions of the people who rejected us don't matter, then we don't have to believe that the things they think of us are true. When we tell ourselves we didn't want to be a part of a group or a situation, then we don't have to feel that we are missing out. While minimization isn't always an effective technique, it works particularly well when dealing with rejection, because it allows us to put the rejection in its place and move on with increased confidence.

However, you have to be very careful with this approach. Minimization can be a tricky tightrope to walk. If you use this technique too much, you avoid learning any potential lessons hidden in the rejection. There's a fine line between minimizing how much you wanted something or the insights and opinions of the people who rejected you, and denial.

If you're turned down for a promotion and your boss provides you with feedback on why, that's an opportunity to face some truths and develop a personal improvement plan. If you minimize the feedback and do nothing with it, what are the chances you'll be ready for the next career opportunity? The same is true in personal relationships. People who can't sustain relationships often live in denial, minimizing the feedback they get from people they care about regarding their role in the failure of the relationship. A little minimization is healthy for handling rejection, but denial is unhelpful, so stay on the healthy side of the line.

Minimization can also sound like sour grapes, if you practice it in front of other people, so it might be best to keep it to yourself. Use minimization, but listen to any direct feedback you're given and use it as a path forward, to prepare yourself for the next opportunity to achieve your goals in career or life.

What techniques can you use to minimize the importance of rejection?

1) **Put their judgment in perspective.** Pull out a journal or a piece of paper and start writing about the person or people who rejected you. Make a note of why the opinion of whoever rejected you isn't the most important opinion in the world (because let's be honest: usually, it isn't). Are there other people whose opinion is more important, even if you don't know them yet? People are fallible and make mistakes, and reminding yourself that the person or people who rejected you could have made a mistake is a great way to minimize how much the rejection stings.

2) **Reframe the desire.** In that same journal or sheet of paper, see if you can reframe how much you wanted what you didn't get. Usually, one rejection opens the door to other possibilities. Think about opportunities you can now pursue because you have been freed up by the rejection. Are the other opportunities for you, even though this one didn't work out? And could those other opportunities turn out even **better**?

3) **Don't float down the river in Egypt.** Too much minimization can turn into denial, which is unhealthy and inhibits future growth. We often don't recognize our own denial, so recruit someone close to you to provide a reality check. Use a friend or family member as a sounding board, and ask them to let you know if you have crossed the fine line between healthy minimization of the issue, into outright denial.

LEADER'S
Toolbox

Helping Your Employees
Manage Rejection

LEADERS OFTEN HAVE TO HELP THEIR EMPLOYEES MANAGE rejection. Perhaps they didn't get a promotion they had been hoping for, or a choice assignment to work on a prestigious project. In some fields, like sales, your employees may be getting rejected all the time! How leaders talk to their teams about rejection can play a big role in whether or not the employees are able to shake it off and remain energized about their work.

Remind your employees that rejection isn't personal. If they didn't get a promotion, point out one specific element of the winning candidate's background that sealed the hiring decision. Research on explanatory style suggests that when people can see a quantifiable reason for something to have happened, they take it less personally. If you can frame the decision like, "the other candidate had this one thing going for them—this degree, experience in this area, etc. Work on that, and you'll be a stronger candidate in the future," the rejection won't feel as personal.

Another thing that makes rejection sting a little less for your employees is refocusing them on their strengths and successes. If a salesperson missed a goal, don't just **tell** him he'll do better next time. Point him toward prospects that have been successful for him in the past. Set him up to actually **do** better, and explain your reasoning for refocusing him as you do it, so he learns how to proactively bounce back from rejection on his own. Similarly, if an employee feels rejected for a raise or promotion, you can bring back her self-esteem by giving her projects that align with her natural strengths. When you allow someone to succeed, you are rebuilding their self-efficacy while at the same time giving them a healthy distraction from feelings of rejection.

Strategy: Distract Yourself

This is your brain on rejection: *"I just got rejected from the most important thing in my life. Nothing else matters but this."*

This is what you want your brain to say, instead: *"It doesn't matter nearly as much as X."*

Abby had no idea what she would do next. Two years ago she left her family and her job back in the Midwest to move out here with Josh. She thought he would be proposing soon. Instead, he told her last week that their relationship was getting "too hard" and "they just weren't having any fun together any more."

As she moved boxes into her tiny new apartment, Abby's eyes stung with tears. She couldn't bear to look at the box with photos in it—every single photo had Josh in it. In fact, almost everything in her apartment reminded her of him. They had been together for six years, and nearly everything she owned was tied to some memory of him. She kept thinking that any minute now her phone would ring and he would be on the other end of the line, telling her he had made a grave mistake and that she should come back.

There was a knock on the door. Abby jumped up and wiped her eyes with the backs of her hands as she answered.

It wasn't Josh. It was her friend Caroline, with a bottle of pre-mixed Sangria. Caroline plopped to the floor in front of an open box, and grabbed two glasses out.

"Have a drink, then come with me to the show!" Caroline pleaded.

"Look, Caroline, I know I told you I'd go, but I can't now," Abby replied.

"You CAN. And you should. We need a keyboard player anyway. Maybe you can get up and play with us. I'm not taking no for an answer."

Abby somehow found herself dressed and sitting behind a keyboard 40 minutes later. Caroline must be magic, she thought. Then she shook her head and focused on the music in front of her. In 10 minutes, the show was going to start and she was going to have to wing it in front of an audience of 200. It had been years since Abby sat in front of a keyboard. Josh had never liked her going out to bars and clubs late at night to play, so she gradually stopped.

As the lights came up and Abby started to play, she saw nothing in her mind but the keys in front of her. There was nothing in her head but the music. For the first time in a long time, she felt like herself.

The last resilience technique for rejection is distraction. When dealing with other struggles, distraction is usually considered an unhelpful technique, as avoiding problems isn't usually recommended. But when it comes to rejection, distraction is actually one of the most useful strategies there is. While the previous technique, "it wasn't that great anyway," was all about minimizing the importance of the thing you didn't get or can't have, this technique is about refocusing your attention on something you **can** have, and making **that** be the thing that matters to you.

Salespeople regularly use a tactic called "attentional deployment" to reduce anxiety over making sales calls, where they shift their attention away from the possibility of hearing "no" from their clients, and instead focus on anything else during the conversation. Distracting yourself following a rejection works in a similar way, because not only does it lessen the immediate pain, it also gives you a healthy activity to shift your focus and energy to, moving forward.

By distracting yourself from the situation, you are able to avoid the most common and harmful pitfall associated with rejection: rumination. Rumination is a hyper-focus on the past, and it fills our brains with negative thoughts. Often when we're rejected, we can't help but replay the situation over and over in our heads. In order to move forward into the future, we need to replace those negative, ruminating thoughts with something else. While it may be hard at first, if you start small, you'll find that you can distract yourself from getting caught in the cycle of rumination. When you distract yourself with thoughts of anything besides the rejection, you train your brain to refocus.

What techniques are the most successful at distracting yourself from the sting of rejection?

1. **Snap the rubber band.** I know one person who gets over the pain of a breakup by snapping a rubber band on her wrist. Come up with at least one small habit you can use in a moment when you feel yourself dwelling on rejection, to distract your mind from rejection. Use that habit to banish any obtrusive thoughts of rejection that enter your mind.

2. **Find a new love.** Pick up a hobby you enjoy, and spend your free time becoming a master of the subject. Fill your hours with friends and family. Go on a trip. When we distract ourselves with another activity, we are diminishing the importance of the rejection in our lives. We are not only mentally reducing it to a smaller place, but we're replacing those hours in a day that we might otherwise be ruminating, with a constructive activity.

A Final Thought About Surviving Rejection

Rejection causes us pain, so it's natural to want to avoid it. But when we fear rejection, we risk playing our lives on a small scale to avoid failure, embarrassment, or hurt. To be successful in life, we have to be willing to risk a little rejection along the way! When we are able to tell ourselves, "It isn't personal, it wasn't that great anyway, and it doesn't matter to me," we allow ourselves the freedom we need to move on from rejection.

To shift your perspective from the personal, try:

- Catching your inner voice telling you that the rejection is personal, and correcting it

- Reflecting on your past successes

- Surrounding yourself with people who appreciate you

To minimize the importance of the rejection, try:

- Questioning the judgment of the people who rejected you

- Reframing how much you wanted what you can't have

- Being careful! Too much of this technique can turn into denial

To distract yourself, try:

- Practicing attentional deployment to avoid short-term rumination

- Taking up long-term hobbies and finding other places to direct your time and attention

DEALING WITH ILLNESS AND INJURY

I DIDN'T PLAN TO LET CANCER BRING ME DOWN FOR LONG. ABOUT a year after the original diagnosis, I felt like my life was starting to come together again. So it came as a big blow when I looked down one summer morning and saw a spot on my left thigh. It was tiny, but an ominous black color. I knew it was bad news.

The doctor biopsied it and put a rush on the pathology report. It was, indeed, another melanoma. I reeled at the thought that my cancer had tried to come back. But there was good news, too: I caught it so early that it was stage 0. My doctor said almost no one would have noticed it, and that I found it so early because I had been vigilant. I had saved my own life, this time.

I looked forward to celebrating five years cancer-free, which is a milestone for cancer survivors, because survival rates go up and chances of recurrence go down. For my five-year visit to the cancer hospital, I asked my doctor to schedule me for a full battery of tests and scans. "Not because I think there's anything there. I believe you when you tell me there's no metastatic disease. But we talked about doing it to get a baseline, in case the cancer comes back years from now."

"Baseline," he repeated. "Yes, as long as you understand we'd just be getting a baseline. We're not looking for any cancer." And he sent me for the scans.

When the hospital called me back 14 days later, I was surprised to hear his voice on the other end of the line. In the cancer world, usually the nurse calls with the good news, and the bad news is left to the doctor to deliver. But we hadn't even been looking for bad news—I couldn't imagine what he could have called to say.

"Courtney, there's no cancer."

I felt the lump in my throat start to disappear.

"There's no cancer. But…" The pause seemed to go on forever. "We found an aneurysm in your brain. It's called an arteriovenous malformation. It could be about to hemorrhage. I can't believe this. It's completely unrelated to the cancer, but we never would have found it."

Five years after beating cancer, I had an aneurysm in my brain. By this time, I was married. I was running a small nonprofit out of my living room. My husband and I had started mentoring a teenaged boy we would go on to adopt. This couldn't be happening.

But it was. Within three weeks, I had packed up my life into one giant box and a giant suitcase, and moved to New York City for several months, where I underwent three brain surgeries. The third surgery was a full open craniotomy, where doctors opened my skull and removed nine cubic centimeters of brain that was being compromised by the tangle of blood vessels.

When I woke up from surgery, the first thing I saw were doctors holding fingers in my face. I tried to open my eyes more, but the pain made my vision like an angry red blanket. "Three fingers," I muttered, wanting to go back to sleep. The doctors exclaimed that I hadn't lost any of my vision, which was almost miraculous. I slept until that afternoon, when the nurse woke me up to try to get me to walk. I assumed that getting out of bed and stretching my legs would feel good. I was wrong. I could barely make it to the door without collapsing. For days my brand-new husband of only 10 months stood by my side and tried to encourage me to take just a few more steps. When I was too exhausted to go any further, I lay back in bed, but I couldn't even pick up a book and read because the words seemed to swim in front of me. I could see, but somehow my eyes just weren't able to focus on words. My whole life, reading had always been my escape, the thing I was best at. Now I couldn't even read.

WHEN OUR LIFE OR HEALTH IS THREATENED, IT CAN BE TEMPTing to panic. Although we know in our heads that none of us have forever to live, it's much easier to make it through the day if we don't focus on that fact! So we go on about our lives as though this day is one in a long line of days we'll have to accomplish whatever we want to accomplish. We fill our lives with work, family, friends, community. With things that matter and things that don't. And then when that life is threatened, we feel shocked.

In the moment we realize our mortality, the things that matter to us can often come into clearer focus. Something we wanted to accomplish but had forgotten about. People we want to spend more time with. The important things in life can sometimes appear, crystal clear in front of us. On the other hand, the threat to our very existence can sometimes send us into a tailspin. We want to do **everything** while we still have time, and every potential lost opportunity is of equal importance.

With our lives and well-being at stake, we are likely to either go into shock, denial, or panic mode, none of which are conducive to making smart, life-saving decisions. Our behavior in those moments sets the stage for how we are going to be able to ultimately find normalcy and enjoy that life, for as long as we continue to have it. In this chapter, I'm going to provide you with techniques to face your mortality and your "new normal" with grace and possibility, so you can adapt to your struggle and regain your balance.

Survival Mode Doesn't Always Help You Survive

More than half of the people in the United States will go through a physical trauma during their life, whether due to illness, accident, assault, or military combat. Many of those individuals will struggle to recover emotionally, according to research.

George MacDonald famously said, "You do not **have** a soul. You **are** a soul. You **have** a body." Those words carry an implication that what happens to your soul must therefore be much more important than what happens to your body. When we face illness or injury, however, we find that it isn't so easy to discount the experiences of our body.

In fact, many of the other challenges in this book can be managed using both task-oriented and emotion-oriented coping skills, often in tandem with one another. With many physical challenges, however, no task-oriented problem solving will work. The problem isn't "fixable" in the traditional sense. Research suggests, therefore, that when dealing with illness or injury, you are more likely to have to turn primarily (or even exclusively) to emotion-focused coping skills than when facing other challenges.

When faced with a physical challenge that cannot be fixed or altered, it is easy for you to believe there is nothing we can do. Your life will never be the same, and you feel like all control has been taken away from you. At times like that, when you face illness and injury, you are at risk for experiencing hopelessness and depression. If you are battling feelings of powerlessness, flip to the first chapter in this book and work on tactics to regain your sense of control and power. If you believe that your new life, with the changes brought on by the illness or injury, has no value, it can be impossible to move forward. Work through that chapter and then come back here with newfound interest in making this life, your new life, full and worthwhile.

When we decide to move positively in the direction of our "new normal" during and immediately following an illness or injury, our thoughts can sometimes work against us. Two traps are very common in this stage: rumination and avoidance. As I've explained in past chapters, rumination is the continual replaying of an event in your head. Rumination is a trap that should be avoided, because it has almost no positive outcomes.

Individuals facing illness and injury can also be prone to avoidance. Sometimes avoidance feels healthy, because it causes us to ignore our challenges and display outwardly positive emotions. But avoidance is impossible to keep up in the long-term, because reality will always creep in. When it does, people who have been relying on avoidance as a coping tool will come crashing back to earth painfully.

It's hard to say that there's a "right" way to act when your life is threatened. No one wants to point fingers at a hospital patient, a survivor, or anyone physically ill or injured and say, "You're not doing this right." Yet research suggests that there are ways to deal with life's physical challenges that are more appropriate and helpful, and other coping mechanisms that are destructive to recovery.

Strategy: Positive Acceptance

My friend Ruben was a great role model throughout his battle with cancer. He had been diagnosed years before I met him, with a kind of blood cancer that is normally considered curable. Ruben, however, had failed treatment after treatment. The best the doctors had been able to do was get his cancer to stop growing, but they couldn't make it disappear. By the time I met him, Ruben had been living with cancer for almost a decade.

As a young adult living with the constant shadow of cancer, Ruben could have been bitter. There were dozens – hundreds! – of things in this world he might not get enough time to experience. But Ruben never focused on those things. Instead, he set his sights on achieving the one single thing he wanted most in the world: to fall in love and get married.

I was lucky to be there the night it happened. I invited Ruben to my 30th birthday party, where he met my friend Jen. They fell quickly in love, and were so happy with life. They were even happy despite the news they received a few months into their relationship: that Ruben's tumor was growing again. All through the planning, Ruben was determined to focus on the amazing gift he had been given: he had found the love of his life. He couldn't worry about what would happen next.

Ruben and Jen enjoyed 11 months of marriage before Ruben succumbed to his cancer. Through it all, he never seemed angry that he had fought so hard to find love, only to have it last so briefly. He had known going in, as had Jen, that they might not have a lot of time. But what they had was worth the fight.

What Ruben embodied in his struggle was acceptance. Acceptance, coming to terms with what is happening to you, is helpful when used in the early stages of recovering from a physical challenge. Research suggests that early acceptance of the situation is one of the healthiest things that someone facing a physical struggle can do. Acceptance involves recognizing and consenting to the changes that have come as a result of your illness or injury.

Acceptance is a complicated tactic, however, because acceptance can either be positive or negative. Positive acceptance looks like: "This situation has happened, the past is the past, I can't change it, so now I will move on and make the most of what my life has to offer." Negative acceptance looks more like: "I guess I'm resigned to my fate. There's nothing I can do." Resigned or passive acceptance is strongly correlated to helplessness, which is a trap you want to avoid.

Your life may never be the same. But that doesn't automatically mean it has to be worse. Reframing your current situation as "the new normal" instead of thinking of it as the aftermath of a traumatic situation may help you put one foot in front of the other and carry on down your new path.

Some research suggests that a very small amount of avoidance – like pretending you aren't facing a physical struggle or wishing everything was back to normal – can be helpful very early in the coping process, if the reality of the physical challenge is too overwhelming. For example, if avoidance helps a person stay positive in the very first few days of a painful hospital stay, it might be useful. Long-term avoidance, however, will block you from accomplishing the other three techniques in this section, which are critical to being able to move forward. For instance, drug and alcohol dependence can be forms of long-term avoidance. Avoidance does more harm than good, and if used, should be dropped as quickly as possible.

Finding acceptance is a crucial first step when facing illness and injury, because it paves the way for the other coping techniques to come. Illness and injury can have a way of making you wish you could do things differently, or live someone else's life. Acceptance will allow you to move out of a past that is no longer yours, and into the future.

What techniques allow us to find positive acceptance of an illness or injury?

1. **Embrace the "new normal."** When your current circumstances don't resemble the life you had previously worked hard to build, it can be hard not to feel resentful and angry. You can manage those feelings by finding elements of your new normal to appreciate. If

there are activities from before that are still available to you, get back out there and participate. Don't let old hobbies or old friendships drift away if they still have value to you, just because you might feel like a different person. Make whatever modifications you need to, in order to be able to enjoy the things you have always loved. Many of us who have coped with illness and injury also report finding more time and energy for activities we always wanted to try but kept putting off. Once you realize life is short, you might feel compelled to try new things. By keeping elements of the old and adding new adventures, your new normal may end up being more enjoyable than your old normal, anyway!

2. **Avoid avoidance.** Recovering from an illness or injury requires a dose of reality that may not always be comfortable. Have honest conversations with your doctors and others who have faced a similar struggle, to get an accurate picture of what recovery and life will be like for you. There's no need to scare yourself with worst-case scenarios and what-if's, but conversations with professionals and other survivors will help you avoid avoidance and face reality in a healthy way.

Strategy: Find Support

The pleading tone was unmistakable, even over email.

When Amy opened the email, she could tell the woman on the other end needed help. Amy was used to getting emails like this; as a volunteer for a miscarriage and pregnancy loss support organization, she fielded distraught emails from both women and men several times a week.

"I feel like I'm going crazy," the email from the woman named Candace stated. "Nobody seems to understand. They just keep telling me to try again. But I have been trying, and I've lost three babies. My body is betraying me. Why don't they understand?"

Amy understood. Four years earlier, she had been where Candace was. She had lost a pregnancy at the end of the first trimester, and everyone around her was trying to be supportive. "You can try again," they said. "It's God's plan," they said. "You just need to stop being so stressed and it'll happen," they said. Even her husband didn't really get it. He had comforted himself with statistics on how common miscarriage is, but Amy didn't want the statistics. She had wanted someone to recognize that she had been carrying a baby, and the loss of that baby was catastrophic to her.

Amy started to type a message back to Candace. "Please come join our group," she wrote. "We have all been where you are. No one here will think you are strange, or grieving too hard, or just need to move on. We all **do** move on to have happy lives and hopefully healthy pregnancies, but if you come here you'll be with people who understand what that process looks like, because it doesn't happen right away."

One of the tactics that works best immediately following a physical struggle is social support. Many studies have found that strong social and personal networks are a key factor in healthy psychological recovery. Social support works to help us heal because it keeps us engaged with the world around us. Also, communicating with our friends and family can be a healthy outlet for emotional expression. In one study, social support as a coping mechanism following cancer led to greater inner peace among the study participants.

When looking for social support during an illness or injury, your friends and family are an obvious place to turn. They are likely already right by your side, helping you with your survival. In fact, one of the benefits that physical challenges have compared to some of the other challenges in this book is that by their very nature, physical struggles are visible and obvious to others, and they draw your loved ones to your presence. As opposed to other challenges, which can be invisible to others, you might not even need to ask the people close to you to come and support you—many may already be there, ready to help with whatever you ask.

Another great place to find emotional support is through a group of like-minded people going through a similar experience, as Amy was suggesting to Candace. When I was diagnosed, I found an online community of young adults with cancer, and started talking to other young people about what it was like to face a life-threatening diagnosis so young. I loved the group so much that after I went into remission, I got a job there! People in support networks don't know and love you like your existing friends and family, but they have the benefit of having been there and done that, so they bring a different type of support to you. Having other people to talk to who have walked the same path is a surefire way to reduce the isolation and confusion of a physical challenge.

Interestingly, no matter your personality or what physical challenge you are facing, getting support from those around you is instrumental in your ability to move forward.

What techniques help us connect and communicate to find support?

1. **Turn to friends and family.** When receiving support from friends and family, it can help to tell them what you need. Some people may try to give you facts and figures about your recovery. To avoid uncomfortable situations like this, be up front with your loved ones about what kind of conversations you are looking for. Remind them that you may have to discuss things that are painful for them to hear (because they love you and they're scared, too!), but that you need them to be supportive listeners. Take the lead and direct the conversation to the things that will be most helpful to you, and be honest about what types of topics you'd rather avoid right now. In doing

that, you'll be setting them up for success to be the best possible support network for you.

2. **Find a group.** Support groups of every type exist for nearly every injury, illness, or trauma you might face, and they are a great place to connect with other people sharing your same experience. Maybe you aren't a person for whom socializing and engagement come naturally. You might be thinking that this is a coping tactic you'd rather avoid, but research suggests you think again because social support works for everyone. Now, how you seek social support is up to you. You might prefer your social support online rather than face-to-face. Or you might be better one-on-one versus in a group. Whether you are an introvert or an extrovert, those struggling with illness or injury find greater inner peace and have an easier time moving forward when they reach out to those around them.

Strategy: Focus on What You Can Fix

From his hospital bed, Marshall was researching carbon fiber finishes and suction sealing. The options for replacement legs were more plentiful than he might have guessed.

His doctors were amazed at how well he was doing just a month out from a terrible car accident. He had lost his left leg above the knee, and was looking into his options for a prosthetic leg. Life as an amputee would be a huge change for Marshall: he had previously played soccer most weekends with the guys and was training for a half-marathon with his girlfriend.

Marshall's mom was holding his hand when the doctors brought in the first of the brochures to discuss his options for the prosthesis. She was scared for him, because she had read about the pain many amputees experience getting used to a prosthesis. She and Marshall had talked about how difficult the therapy would be, but Marshall

LEADER'S
Toolbox

When Your Team Members
Face Illness or Injury

MANAGING SOMEONE WHO IS GOING THROUGH ILLNESS or injury can be difficult in a variety of ways. Managers often report not knowing what to say or do for their employees who are facing physical struggles. You might worry that your employee would feel uncomfortable talking about their illness or injury, so you don't want to ask. Or you might worry that if you **don't** say anything, they'll think you're callous and uncaring!

It can feel impossible to know the "right" way to behave as the manager of someone going through an illness or injury. The bad news is that because everyone is different, there is no right way to handle the situation. The good news is that there's a simple, single solution: ask.

Ask your employee:

- "How can I best support you as you are going through this?"

- "What are your plans for what I know will be a difficult juggle between your work and your health, and how can I help you accomplish that?"

- "Is there anything you would like me to say – or not say – to the rest of the team when they ask about how you are doing?"

By letting the employee take the lead, you are avoiding the common pitfalls of uncomfortable conversation when it comes to things like time off, the spread of private health information, or simply how much they want your support.

was focusing his attention on learning everything he could about the types of prosthetic devices, and choosing the best one for him.

Marshall hadn't been able to control losing his leg in the accident. But he could control which replacement leg he was going to get, and he was determined to choose wisely. He was controlling what he could.

Once your social support systems are in place and you have begun accepting the "new normal" of your life, many people adapting after a physical challenge turn to problem-focused coping. Problem-focused coping relies on fixing what can be fixed, and doing what can be done. There isn't always something that can be done when the struggle is physical, which risks those feelings of helplessness we're trying to avoid. But often, even in the most critical of situations, there is still a way to use problem-focused coping to help you regain your balance.

Problem-focused coping strategies, as we discussed at the very beginning of the book, include gathering information, making important decisions, incorporating necessary life changes to adapt to your new normal—anything that is task-oriented. What can be done about your situation? What decisions need to be made?

Watch out for two things when beginning the information-gathering phase: starting too early, and doing too much. Task-oriented strategies seem to work best a little bit later in the process, after the social support and acceptance tactics are already in place. In fact, if you try to use problem-focused coping too early, some research suggests you might experience "information overload," and it will work against you, instead of for you.

If you fall into the information overload trap, you can also get stuck in that rumination and helplessness cycle. Don't stay here for long! A great technique for getting out of the pit of rumination is refocusing on a positive goal. When you set a goal, your eye is automatically on the future, making obsessive thinking about the past impossible. Try to set a goal that isn't directly related to your physical struggle, but something separate, perhaps something you have wanted to accomplish for awhile. Setting and accomplishing goals is a great way to bring your attention to the here and now.

One of the reasons that problem-oriented coping can help you cope with your illness or injury is that solving problems helps you combat those feelings of powerlessness. Goal-setting can be an important part of reclaiming your power and moving on with your life. But perhaps your old goals aren't realistic anymore, or perhaps your focus has changed since your illness or injury, and the old goals aren't important in the same way. Setting new goals is a healthy way to not only take action, but also to mark a new beginning of this phase of your life.

There may not be many ways for you to feel like you are taking action and making progress right now. But as you move through your illness or injury, there will still be ways you can make progress and solve problems, and each time you do, you gain the emotional strength and control you are craving.

What techniques are successful at focusing your perspective on what you can fix?

1. **Avoid information overload.** Gathering too much information can lead to "analysis paralysis." Resist the urge to stay up late at night Googling symptoms, outcomes, or horror stories. The line between the perfect amount of information and information overload is different for everyone, so there isn't a clear-cut way to know if you've crossed the line. But one thing to look out for is whether or not the information you are gathering has an end goal. If you are gathering information to make a specific decision, it is more likely to be healthy information-gathering. If you have made your decisions, but you're still scouring the Internet to either prove or disprove your choice, you've crossed the line into an unhealthy tactic. Information should make you feel empowered, not afraid.

2. **Aim high.** Goal setting can be critical in helping you reclaim your power after an illness or injury. You may have some previous goals that are no longer realistic, or perhaps your priorities have shifted. When you set new goals, you take concrete action in a situation that might otherwise make you feel powerless.

Strategy: Find Meaning in the Struggle

Finally, meaning-making also seems to be an important technique for struggling with physical challenges. Meaning-making asks the question, "What is the purpose of this event in my life?" and it often drives the experience of growth and peace that is known to happen after a life- and health-threatening event. This "post traumatic growth," as it is known, only comes to fruition when we put into perspective our challenges and choose to grow from them by making meaning of the situation. Making meaning out of challenge also relates strongly to optimism, which studies show is important for recovery. An optimistic view of a physical challenge means experiencing thoughts like: "It could be worse," or "At least I still…" Research suggests that when we reach the stage of making meaning out of our physical challenge, we have fully integrated the event into our lives and are ready to move forward.

Struggle doesn't always have to separate us from who we used to be—sometimes it can bring us closer to who we are trying to become. When you think about why you are facing this struggle, know that many people come out of situations like this feeling stronger, more powerful, and more positive about their lives.

An incredibly effective way to get meaning out of a physical challenge is through volunteerism. Giving back to help someone else, particularly someone struggling with what you went through, allows you to become a hero for someone else, and it makes your struggle purposeful. Helping someone else is one of the best ways to gain perspective following a struggle. It's one thing to just survive. But the ultimate end of the healing journey isn't survival. It's actually reaching back behind you and extending a hand to someone else. When we do, we often find our struggle has greater meaning.

Physical challenges can alter your life in an instant. When I was diagnosed with cancer at age 26, I didn't realize at the time that I might never have children. While the cancer didn't render me physically incapable of having children, pregnancy would put me at greater risk of recurrence. After lots of soul-searching, I decided I would never take that risk. I might never be a mother.

I threw all my maternal energy into starting up a nonprofit, which became like a baby to me. One month at a volunteer event, my husband and I met a bright young man who peppered me with questions about how to get into a college music program, after hearing that I had once been a college music major, myself. He had admirable goals of getting a college degree and becoming a successful musician. He explained to me that he had been practically supporting himself since junior high school, with the goal of escaping poverty and pursuing his dreams of a music career.

I spent plenty of time with Anthony that night, answering his questions on what college music programs are like and how he could improve his chances of getting in and, ultimately, graduating.

How could I have known, at the time, that the young man I was having a simple conversation with would become my son?

The following week Anthony came over for pizza, toting his college applications. We worked through the evening, excitedly planning for his future. He started coming over every week to work on his essays. By spring semester, he was over at our house twice a week—once we worked on his essay-writing, and the other visit we took him to an SAT tutor we found for him. When we finally made the long-awaited drive to drop him off at college, he presented us with a "University of North Texas Mom" shirt for me, and a "University of North Texas Dad" shirt for my husband.

Anthony is now our legally adopted son. He may not look like me. He may not have been what I was expecting. But he is the child I was meant to be a mother to. Everything I went through as a 26 year old with cancer brought me to the place where, just a few years later, I would become Mom to a teenager in need.

Illness and injury can provide us with opportunities we never would have been aware of had we stayed in our healthy, safe cocoon. When we grab on to those opportunities, we are likely to notice something beneficial in our new situations. Viktor Frankl's book *Man's Search for Meaning* is regarded as one of the key books on surviving trauma. Frankl believes that it is natural to ask the question, "Why is this happening to me?!?!" We want to understand why we had to struggle, and we look for the greater context. Often the meaning of our struggle isn't obvious. But if your goal is to come out of your struggle strong (and maybe even stronger than before!), then finding meaning in the struggle is a very important tactic to use.

A man in the audience at one of my presentations raised his hand when I was taking questions. He told the group how he had been diagnosed with multiple sclerosis when his youngest child was only four. "I became helpless around the house those first years," he said. "It was embarrassing. I didn't want my kids to see me sick. But then I realized that I was getting time at home while they were little, and I would have never gotten that chance before. Now I get to spend time being a dad who reads them books. I know all their friends' names. If I hadn't gotten sick, I wouldn't have been that kind of dad." Those who can find a meaning and a benefit in illness or injury are not only able to cope, but often emerge from their struggle even stronger and more successful than before.

What techniques help you see a greater meaning in your illness or injury?

1. **Find a purpose.** Journaling is a great technique for making meaning out of struggles, because it requires reflection. Pick up a journal and start writing: How could this physical challenge end up contributing to your life, instead of detracting from it? How could this experience add value to you, and how could you, in turn, add value to the world because of this? How could your worldview shift for the better because of your experience? What do you know now that you could teach someone else?

2. **Be a hero.** Volunteerism is one of the most effective techniques at helping those of us who have been through trauma find perspective. In my book *The Giving Prescription*, I lay out a plan for using philanthropy and volunteerism to recover from life-changing situations like illness and injury. The key is this: find something meaningful to you. It can be related to your own ill-

ness or injury, or something entirely separate. Find a way to contribute that speaks to you. If you like speaking up for others, become an advocate. If you like giving guidance, be a mentor. Offer up whatever time, talent, and treasure you have to give to a cause that feels meaningful. When you give back to someone else, you regain the personal power you may feel has been missing since your illness and injury.

A Final Word About Dealing with Illness and Injury

As you move forward from your physical challenge, remember to give yourself plenty of time to work through these four strategies. There isn't a time clock on this process, and everyone's time frame is different. At whatever speed you take them, the techniques in this chapter are the most helpful for overcoming a physical challenge life throws in your path.

The four steps to moving forward after an illness or injury are:

- First, use positive acceptance to come to grips with your new normal

- Second, use social support to keep you engaged and offer you opportunities to communicate what you are going through

- Next, focus on what you can fix by gathering information, making decisions, and regaining a measure of control

- Finally, find meaning in the struggle by helping others and discovering a greater purpose your injury or illness might serve

GO FORTH...
TO STRUGGLE
SUCCESSFULLY!

WHEN FACING STRUGGLE AND STRESS IN OUR LIVES, SOME OF US pause and wonder "What do I do now?" Others of us barrel right on through the challenge without stopping for air. Whichever type you are, you've hopefully found relief within these pages. For each of the struggles in your life, your work, and your home, there is a proven set of corresponding behaviors that will do two things:

- Relieve the discomfort and psychological burden of the struggle

- Help you move forward past the struggle

Some of the tactics you're getting ready to use are more obviously aimed at helping you manage your emotions. Stressful situations often can't change until we reduce their psychological impact, taking them from giant, intimidating forces in our lives to manageable moments. At the same time you are changing how you emotionally respond to the struggle, other techniques are great at helping you move forward past the struggle. The more problem-solving techniques are obviously focused on solutions and actions, and through those tactics you can see the light at the end of the tunnel, and try to put an end to the stressful situation.

You may have noticed that often the two techniques go hand-in-hand. While you are tactically trying to solve problems and move past the struggle, you are automatically reducing its emotional significance to you. Many of the steps you can take to get an emotional toehold on a problem by their very nature make you more able to put the struggle behind you and move forward. So in attacking the problem from one angle, you naturally attack from the other.

Sharing What You've Learned

Now that you've finished the book, you know how to best handle each of the six states of struggle. Now you want to share your wisdom with your friends and family, right?

Not so fast.

You can't solve someone else's struggle for them. When we think we know how to help someone solve their problem, it can be tempting to step in. We want to share our knowledge and be helpful. But often, other people don't want "help" when they're struggling. In the middle of a tough time, "help" seems like "advice" which seems like "bossiness" or "lip service." People who are struggling just brush that off.

No matter how much you may want to assist your friend or loved one in overcoming their struggle, they have to do it themselves. Otherwise the recipient of your advice might be sitting there thinking, "You don't know what I'm dealing with. You think you know, but you don't." When you step in and try to tell someone what to do, you risk alienating them at the time they actually need you most.

So what **can** you do? If your friend, colleague or loved one is struggling, first listen and ask questions. Even if you feel like you've been in this exact same position before, ask them clarifying questions about what's going on. Questions like, "When did this start happening?" and "What are you experiencing when this goes on?" will get them talking. And remember, just having someone to talk to is an important coping technique for many of the types of struggle! As they talk, reflect what they are saying back to them. It might feel cheesy to say things like, "So I hear you saying…" so if that's too therapist-speak for you, try something like, "Oh man, I can understand why you felt X when Y was happening."

Next, it's best to resist the urge to give direct advice. When I jumped right in to parenting a teenager, I discovered an interesting phenomenon. Anthony hadn't had a lot of people to turn to for advice and support in his life, so when I first became his mom, he called me all the time asking for guidance. For the first year or so, he listened to everything I said with rapt attention. He was so happy to have people to share in his decision-making, I think sometimes he even texted me to ask what he should have for lunch! But by the end of his sophomore year in college, something had changed. He'd still call to ask for my advice, but the response would be different. Now, he'd shoot my ideas down. "That's never going to work, Mom." "See, that's a bad idea, because…" Everything I said was "dumb," "wouldn't work," or else I "don't understand college kids." I seemed to have gotten stupid overnight (but if you have teenagers, you've probably gotten stupid at giving advice, too).

One day I tried a different tactic. He called in a panic, worried that a degree in music performance and composition wasn't a sensible decision. "I'll never make any money, Mom. People respect people who make money. Maybe I should study business and have my own business someday, like Dad." My husband freaked out at the thought of him changing majors this late in the game, not to mention abandoning his dream. He wanted to call Anthony right away and tell him no way was he going to change his major! He needed to follow his passion! I asked my husband to let me handle it, and I picked up the phone:

"So you don't feel like music is a sensible career path?"

"Are you worried about money?"

"Oh, so you're concerned that if you're struggling for money, you'll be unhappy."

"You feel like people who don't have to worry about money are happier?"

"That's a really good point, that you wanted to do music because you want to be happy, but you're worried that you need more money to make you happy."

"Actually I just read this fascinating article about how money makes us happy, but only up to a certain dollar amount. Then after that we're no happier. I can't remember the exact dollar amount (okay, I totally could, but I just said that to make him feel less like **I** was the one giving the advice), but do you want me to send you the article? You can look up the dollar amount it says, and then as long as you can find a job making that much money, in whatever field it is, you'll probably be at least as happy as anyone else from the money standpoint."

I sent the article.

He kept studying music.

I have no idea if he ever read the article. But just knowing that some expert, not me, said he didn't need a million dollars to be happy in life did the trick. If I had come back at him with advice from me, he might not have listened. But by showing him research, by making the advice come from an expert, I gave my advice a greater endorsement than just "this is what I think you should do."

If you have a friend who is struggling, **show** them what to do, don't tell them. Photocopy a page from this book and give it to them (it's okay—you have my permission!). Or if you really like the person, let them borrow your copy for a while. Send them online articles about resilience techniques that apply directly to their struggle.

Whatever you do, let them discover this wisdom for themselves, rather than just telling them what to do. It can be tough to bite your tongue when you know you have some knowledge that they'll benefit from, but they have to acquire it on their own, just like you did.

YOU NOW HAVE A LOT OF TOOLS IN YOUR TOOLBOX TO HELP YOU achieve accelerated resilience. You understand better how they work and when they are most useful. My hope is that you'll be able to meet struggle head on with techniques that help you take action, shift your emotions, find perspective, get support, and refocus your mind.

As you put this book down I hope you feel prepared to take on the challenges the world throws at you. If you deploy the strategies in this book when they are called for, you will bounce back from life's struggles more successfully. You will be a more resilient leader, colleague, friend, partner, or parent. Good luck, and please stay in touch. I would love to hear how you've used these techniques to find accelerated resilience.

ACKNOWLEDGEMENTS

I'M SO GRATEFUL TO MY ROCK OF A HUSBAND, JAMIE, WHO IS everything a partner should be. I marvel at the strength of my son, Anthony, who is the best I know at smiling in a rainstorm. And I deeply appreciate the support of my family and friends, who give me guidance, purpose, and love.

I am also thankful to you, dear readers, for the inspiration you provide me. Every one of your stories of success in the face of life's challenges is the fuel to my fire. I wish you strength when you need it, and peace when you don't.

REFERENCES

Chapter 1

Baloglu, Nuri. "The relationship between prospective teachers' strategies for coping with stress and their perceptions of student control." *Social Behavior and Personality* (2008).

Lazarus, Richard S and Susan Folkman. *Stress, Appraisal, and Coping*. Springer Publishing Company, 1984.

Mikulincer, Mario. "Coping and learned helplessness: effects of coping strategies on performance following unsolvable problems." *European Journal of Personality* (1989).

Pillen, MT, Douwe Beijaard, PJ den Brok. "Tension in beginning teachers' professional identity development, accompanying feelings and coping strategies." *European Journal of Teacher Education* (2012): doi: 10.1080/02619768.2012.696192.

Rock, David. "SCARF: A brain-based model for collaborating with and influencing others." *Neuroleadership Journal*. 2008.

Seligman, Martin EP, Steven F Maier, James H Geer. "Alleviation of learned helplessness in the dog." *Journal of Abnormal Psychology* (1968).

Skinner, Ellen A. "A Guide to Constructs of Control." Journal of Personality and Social Psychology (1996).

Sturman, Edward D, Myriam Mongrain, Paul M Kohn. "Attributional Style as a predictor of hopelessness depression." *Journal of Cognitive Psychotherapy* (2006).

Chapter 2

Amiot, Catherine E, Deborah J Terry, Nerina L Jimmieson, Victor J Callan. "A longitudinal investigation of coping processes during a merger: Implications for job satisfaction and organizational identification." *Journal of Management* (2006).

Bernerth, Jeremy B, H Jack Walker, Stanley G Harris. "Change fatigue: Development and initial validation of a new measure." *Work and Stress* (2011): doi: 10.1080/02678373.2011.634280.

Bridges William. *The Way of Transition: Embracing Life's Most Difficult Moments.* Da Capo Press, 2001.

Grdinovac, Jane A, George B Yancey. "How organizational adaptations to recession relate to organizational commitment." *The Psychologist-Manager Journal* 15, no.1 (2012).

Jimmieson, Nerina L, Deborah J Terry, Victor J Callan. "A longitudinal study of employee adaptation to organizational change: The role of change-related information and change-related self-efficacy." *Journal of Occupational Health Psychology* (2004): doi: 10.1037/1076-8998.9.1.11.

Leiter, Michael P, Phyllis Harvie. "Conditions for staff acceptance of organizational change: Burnout as a mediating construct." *Anxiety, Stress, and Coping* (1998): doi 10.1080/10615809808249311.

Sherlock-Storey, Mandi, Mark Moss, Sue Timson. "Brief coaching for resilience during organizational change—an exploratory study." *The Coaching Psychologist* (2013).

Teo, Stephen TT, David Pick, Cameron J Newton, Melissa Yeung, Esther Chang. "Organisational change stressors and nursing job satisfaction: the mediating effect of coping strategies." *Journal of Nursing Management* (2013).

Chapter 3

Chao, Ruth Chiu-Lien. "Managing perceived stress among college students: The roles of social support and dysfunctional coping." *Journal of College Counseling* (2011).

Bakker, Arnold, Ij H. Van Emmerik, Pim van Riet. "How job demands, resources and burnout predict objective performance: A constructive replication." *Anxiety, Stress, & Coping* (2008): doi: 10.1080/10615800801958637.

Hallowell, Edward. "Overloaded circuits: Why smart people underperform." *Harvard Business Review* (2005).

Cornerstone OnDemand, Inc. *The State of Workplace Productivity Report*. Kelton, 2012.

Lazarus, Richard S and Susan Folkman. *Stress, Appraisal, and Coping*. Springer Publishing Company, 1984.

Montero-Marin, Jesus, Javier Prado-Abril, Marcelo Marcos Piva Demarzo, Santiago Gascon, Javier Garcia-Campayo. "Coping with stress and types of burnout: Explanatory power of different coping strategies." *PLOS ONE* (2014): doi: 10.1371/journal.pone.0089090.

Redfern Jones, Jane. "Manage workplace chaos by building your resilience." *Nursing Standard* (2012).

Chapter 4

Amason, Allen C, Kenneth R Thompson, Wayne A Hochwater, Allison W Harrison. "Conflict: An important dimension in successful management teams." *Work & Stress* (1995): doi: 10.1016/0090-2616(95)90069-1.

Friedman, Ray, Simon T Tidd, Seven C Currall, James C Tsai. "What goes around comes around: The impact of personal conflict style on work conflict and stress." *The International Journal of Conflict Management* (2000): doi: 10.1108/eb022834.

Papageorgiou, Costas, Adrian Wells. "An empirical test of a clinical metacognitive model of rumination and depression." *Cognitive Therapy and Research* (2003).

Schabracq, Marc J, Jacques AM Winnubst, Cary L Cooper. *The Handbook of Work and Health Psychology, 2nd ed.* John Wiley and Sons, LTD, 2003.

Schat, Aaron CH, E Kevin Kelloway. "Reducing the adverse consequences of workplace aggression and violence: The buffering effects of organizational support." *Journal of Occupational Health Psychology* (2003): doi: 10.1037/1076-8998.8.2.110.

Chapter 5

Boyd, Nancy G, Jeffrey E Lewin, Jeffrey K Sager. "A model of stress and coping and their influence on individual and organizational outcomes." *Journal of Vocational Behavior* (2009): doi:10.1016/j.jvb.2009.03.010.

Cassey, Phillip, Tim M Blackburn. "Publication and rejection among successful ecologists." *BioScience* (2004).

Cronin, Blaise. "The resilience of rejected manuscripts." *Journal of the American Society for Information Science and Technology* (2012): doi: 10.1002/asi.22794.

Gere, Judith, Geoff MacDonald. "An update of the empirical case for the need to belong." *The Journal of Individual Psychology* (2010).

Chapter 6

Hughes, Virginia. "The Roots of Resilience." *Nature* (2012). Accessed January 7, 2015, http://www.nature.com/news/stress-the-roots-of-resilience-1.11570.

Park, Crystal L, Susan Folkman. "Meaning in the context of stress and coping." *Review of General Psychology* (1997).

Jeavons, Susan, DJD L Horne, Ken Greenwood. "Coping style and psychological trauma after road accidents." *Psychology, Health, & Medicine* (2000): doi: 10.1080/713690183.

Felton, Barbara J, Tracey A Revenson. "Coping with chronic illness: A study of illness controllability and the influence of coping strategies on psychological adjustment." *Journal of Consulting and Clinical Psychology* (1984).

Kildal, Morten, Mimmie Willebrand, Gerhard Anderson, Bengt Gerdin, Lisa Ekselius. "Coping strategies, injury characteristics and long-term outcome after burn injury." *Injury, International Journal of the Care of the Injured* (2005): doi: http://dx.doi.org/10.1016/j.injury.2004.06.013.

Lazarus, Richard S and Susan Folkman. *Stress, Appraisal, and Coping*. Springer Publishing Company, 1984.

Jim, Heather S, Susan S Richardson, Deanna M Golden-Kreutz, Barbara L Andersen. "Strategies used in coping with a cancer diagnosis predict meaning in life for survivors." *Health Psychology* (2006): doi: 10.1037/0278-6133.25.6.753.

Feifel, Herman, Stephen Strack, Vivian Tong Nagy. "Coping strategies and associated features of medically ill patients." *Psychosomatic Medicine* (1987): doi: 10.1097/00006842-198711000-00007.

Hack, Thomas F, Lesley F Degner. "Coping responses following breast cancer diagnosis predict psychological adjustment three years later." *Psycho-Oncology* (2003): doi: 10.1002/pon.739.

ABOUT THE AUTHOR

COURTNEY CLARK IS THE LUCKIEST UNLUCKY person in the world. At age 26, Courtney beat melanoma. But five years post-cancer, routine follow-up scans detected a malformation of the blood vessels in her brain that was close to causing a hemorrhage. The aneurysm, which had shown no symptoms, could have ruptured at any time. Courtney underwent a series of brain surgeries in 2011 to remove the malformation.

Throughout her young adulthood, Courtney was committed to helping others, and in 2009 she founded the nonprofit Austin Involved as a way to connect young professionals to meaningful philanthropic experiences. She completed her master's degree in philanthropy, and her graduate research became the basis of her first book, *The Giving Prescription: A Personal Plan for Healing Through Helping*, published in 2014.

Courtney and her husband, Jamie, continue to be active community volunteers. Their volunteer work led them to grow their family, in fact, when they were introduced to a young high school student with dreams of college and success as a musician. Courtney and Jamie adopted Anthony, who is now a college graduate. The other members of their family all have fur and feathers.

Courtney works with companies, nonprofits, and associations who want to build resilience in their team members so they can handle change and challenge in a fast-paced, evolving marketplace.

She would love to hear from you about how you have found success despite your struggles. Connect with her at *www.CourtneyLClark.com*, or on Facebook at *Facebook.com/CourtneyClarkSpeaker*.